P9-EEG-557

Contents

Eclipse Rich Ajax Platform: Bringing Rich Clients to the Web

by Fabian Lange

Eclipse Rich Ajax Platform (RAP) is a great technology; the only problem is that there is no book available about the technology and how to use it. With this book, I want to fill this gap and show where and how Eclipse RAP can be used.

I would like to thank the whole Eclipse RAP team, especially Frank Appel, for supporting me while writing this book. I spent some time during fall 2007 with Frank and his team trying to convert an Eclipse RCP application with RAP. This is where I got firsthand experience and expert advice on this great technology. Thank you for creating Eclipse RAP and providing me with valuable input.

I want also to thank Apress for allowing me to publish this book, especially Steve Anglin, Sofia Marchant, and Damon Larson for the great professional support during the creation of this book.

Additional thanks go to my employer, codecentric GmbH, and all of my colleagues who supported me in one way or another during the creation of this book. I am very proud of working with such a great team.

Very special thanks go to my lovely wife, Marie: thank you for supporting me in a way no one else could, day and night, encouraging me to write this book. I love you deeply.

Feel free to visit www.rap-book.com or e-mail me at fabian@rap-book.com in case of any questions or comments.

Chapter 1: Rich Clients vs. Web Clients

This chapter describes the properties of *rich clients* and *web clients*, and tries to establish a sound definition of each. The focus is on the differences and characteristics that are important for this book—that is, differences that matter for the Eclipse Rich Ajax Platform (RAP). *Eclipse RAP* combines these technologies, allowing you to create rich web clients from rich clients.

Each of the definitions is structured in three parts:

- *Technical aspects*, which describe the technology and patterns involved or used, and the implications they have.

- *Developer aspects*, which describe key properties, like programming language or tooling.

- *Enterprise aspects*, which basically try to identify why big companies should put money into a technology. Of course, enterprise aspects might be important for end users or in other scenarios as well; however, software and its related costs weigh much more in larger environments. Thus, small differences can impose larger consequences.

The definitions are intended to be generic and valid for all programming languages. However, readers of this book are more likely to be familiar with Java than with any other language, so the examples and references are based on Java.

Note   If you are a developer and are just interested in the RAP technology and how to implement it, you might want to skip directly to Chapter 2; but keep in mind that your customers either might have read this chapter or may need advice on finding a solution based on their requirements. For these reasons, you might want to read this chapter first.

A Rich Client Definition

- *Rich client*: Also knows as a desktop application, native application, thick client, or fat client

Technical Aspects

Typically, applications that are considered rich clients don't run in an emulator or browser, but run natively on the operating system of the user's computer. The majority of these rich clients are written in C++, Java, or .NET. Such rich clients have nearly unrestricted access to system resources like memory, storage, input devices (e.g., keyboard and mouse), and output devices (e.g., printer and screen). Only certain functionality, like modifying memory used by other applications, can be restricted by the operating system to prevent malicious applications compromising the system. This access to many system resources allows the application to perform a wide range of tasks, which include operations that can utilize the CPU completely for a noticeable amount of time (e.g., multimedia editing).

Rich clients offer a large feature set optimized to work on a well-defined range of use cases. Often, these applications contain many more features than the user actually needs to perform her job. The look and feel is often designed to be very similar to the host operating system, which makes it easier for users to learn how to use the application, because they can recognize common usage patterns across different applications.

Another feature of rich clients is extensibility using *plug-ins*. Plug-ins are additions provided by vendors or third parties that are able to hook into APIs provided by the rich client and deliver additional functionality.

Usually, data manipulated with the applications is local. If a network is involved at all, it is often just used to pull data, which is then stored locally for processing and sent back to a server later on. This design allows the application to be used offline without any network connection.

Rich client applications are typically able interact with each other using drag-and-drop functionality or other technologies like Microsoft OLE (for Windows), or Bonobo and KParts (for Linux).

Developer Aspects

From a developer point of view, rich clients are easy to implement, because the programming languages and operating systems are very mature and offer a lot of APIs to develop the required functionality. That means that developers don't have to expend as much effort as they used to, as they can reuse existing or provided functionality and can deal with business logic most of the time. They also have access to advanced tooling that helps with the creation, testing, and installation of rich client applications. As the computers running these applications nowadays are powerful enough to run applications that waste CPU power or memory, developers no longer have to spend large amount of time optimizing applications for lesser CPU or memory usage.

A Java, C++, or .NET developer can develop, test, and maintain an entire application, because there is no second technology involved, which would require a different set of competencies.

In the Java world, there are three main players for creating rich clients:

- Eclipse Rich Client Platform
- NetBeans Platform
- Spring Rich

Enterprise Aspects

Rich clients need to be installed, maintained, and updated on each user's workstation. While solutions exist for managing the application maintenance (like HP OpenView, IBM Tivoli, or Microsoft Systems Management Server), users are almost always able to bypass the mechanisms of these solutions. In extreme situations, outdated software can expose security risks or corrupt data, so it is important to supply users with the most recent version of their applications.

While green IT concepts advertise that end user workstations should be very small to reduce costs and power consumption, rich clients are not ideally designed for this. Rich client applications often need a powerful CPU or a lot of memory, but do not utilize powerful hardware most of the time. To be cost efficient, rich clients would need to move heavy operations to the server side where they can be scaled more efficiently, so that the client computers just need to be capable of handling the few remaining lightweight operations.

In spite of these considerations, software and hardware costs are usually less important than the costs of wasted working time when users have to wait for their applications to respond. In the end, slow applications cost more than what would be spent on enabling users to work as efficiently as possible.

The use of plug-ins with rich clients enables more standardization in a company. It's possible to provide the same foundation application to every department, and, for example, provide sales support for the sales department and financial functionality for accounting using plug-ins. This pattern allows for greater source code reuse than separate applications would.

A Web Client Definition

- *Web client*: Also known as a web application, Internet/intranet application, web user interface, and thin client

Technical Aspects

Contrary to rich clients, web clients do not run on top of the computer operating system, but inside the web browser. This imposes many restrictions on web clients. Components cannot be drawn directly on the screen; instead, HTML and CSS, which are the markup languages a browser is able to understand, have to be used to lay out the application. The original concept of HTML did not include multimedia or a high degree of interactivity, so many of these features have been added with plug-ins. However, for web applications, it is not predictable whether a certain plug-in is installed on the client side and exactly what functionality the plug-in delivers.

Classical web applications use the network heavily, because the browser basically shows a screen that has been created remotely, on the server. This slows down interaction between the user and the application, as each interaction requires a server roundtrip. Additionally, the entire screen must be re-requested from the server on each roundtrip. Implicitly, this already indicates the main disadvantage of web clients: they cannot work without a network connection and are impacted by the quality of service the network connection provides. Even with a fast network, much data is transferred on each request, which reduces application performance.

Usually, it is said that the advantage of web applications is that they are good cross-platform applications. They can often be used on mobile phones and kiosk systems—basically anywhere a web browser is installed. However, this is somewhat true as well for rich clients that, for example, just need a virtual machine, or a recompilation on the target platform to run.

Web clients do not need to be installed on the user's hardware, which makes it possible for users to access the application even on a machine where the application should not or cannot be installed.

Developer Aspects

The main language of web clients is HTML, combined with a bit of CSS for better-looking interfaces. The complete layout of the screens has to be done either by the application developer or a web designer. HTML and

CSS offer only limited support for creating user interfaces that are usable at a variety of screen resolutions and that integrate into the native look and feel of the user's operating system. Additional issues arise from the fact that end users can change many display settings of the browser and have incompatible browsers or browser versions installed.

To enable user interaction with the application, developers need to provide some kind of server-side logic that is able to render the required HTML and deal with the data submitted by the user using HTML forms. This need sparked such lightweight scripting languages as Perl and PHP, which were well suited for this job. However, scripting languages often fail to provide concepts that are required to develop structured and maintainable source code.

From the Java point of view, much effort has been spent to create a sound server-side solution for web applications with the Servlets, JSP, and JSF standards. .NET also provides server-side solutions based on ASP.

Enterprise Aspects

From an enterprise perspective, web clients solve software maintenance issues. A single server installation is used by all corporate users, which improves data integrity. For example, a tax rate change can be deployed once to the server and all bills created with the application on the server will be correct. With rich clients, some users would be able to create bills with an incorrect tax rate from their local machine, because their application won't have been updated yet. But this is only true as long all users have a similar browser setup for corporate use; otherwise, cross-browser issues could interfere with the application.

A further advantage is that sensitive data is stored only on the server, and just the set of data being used by the user is transferred from the central storage over the network.

The network dependency of web clients is of less impact for enterprise applications, as internal networks are fast enough to power many simultaneous users. For users working at a customer's site, these applications were impossible to use in the past; however, nowadays wireless networks enable remote users to work with web clients. Still, the issue of poor-quality wireless networks (or in some places, no network access) remains.

Due to the limited functionality of web clients, many companies are using web clients only for read-only data, like phone books or branch/department information. These types of applications do not need much functionality because data maintenance and updates are usually taken care of directly by superusers on the main databases.

A Rich Web Client Definition

- *Rich web client*: Also known as a rich Internet application, Ajax client, Web 2.0 client, and fat thin client

Technical Aspects

Since the beginning of the Web 2.0 era, many old web client technologies have been evolving quickly and the definition of *web client* has changed fundamentally. The revised usage of JavaScript allows web applications to modify static content and interact with page elements. By using Ajax as a transport protocol for asynchronous requests, it has become possible to interact with the server while staying on the same screen, which means that users can continue to work while the application fetches data or updates parts of its screen based on the outcome of a server-side computation. This basically removes the disadvantage of unresponsive applications that always refresh to load data from the server.

In *rich web clients*, state is not only kept on the server side, but also on client side. Usually, data state is managed on the server side, while application state, which does not need to be persisted longer than a browser session, is handled on the client side. Also, it follows the separation-of-concerns pattern, as user-relevant state is just managed by that user on that user's computer.

While network connection is still critical for rich web clients (or maybe even more critical than for traditional web clients, as in total more requests are made at shorter intervals, which are not very tolerant of timeouts), some solutions are emerging, like Google Gears, that let rich web applications continue to work without a network connection by queuing requests to the server in a local storage.

Some people consider very well-designed applications or applications with visual effects to be rich applications, as it's actually not that easy to decide from a user's point of view what qualifies as a rich web application. As a rule of thumb, you could say the following: *if a web application uses JavaScript to load data asynchronously, it is a rich web application.*

Developer Aspects

Manually creating HTML markup is no longer the main method of designing web applications. JavaScript has taken over the lead role, wrapped by some frameworks that make it similar to a traditional programming language, by dealing with cross-browser issues with HTML, CSS, and JavaScript and providing consistent APIs. Additionally, browser manufacturers have worked on adhering to standards, which guarantee that regardless of the browser used, applications can look and work the same.

While the main programming language for the user interface will be often JavaScript, the sever side just generates basic HTML and serves the data used by the application in XML or JSON.

Still, JavaScript has not gained much more functionality than it had already in traditional web clients, which might prevent some features from being implemented in pure JavaScript. For example, many features require Adobe Flash, which is perhaps the most commonly used plug-in for multimedia functionality. So, in the end, developers of rich web applications often need a broad technology knowledge.

Eclipse RAP and Google Web Toolkit are two frameworks that try to solve server- and client-side programming in pure Java and just generate the appropriate HTML and JavaScript dynamically. This would allow the developers to focus on one development language and environment.

Enterprise Aspects

Rich web clients usually impose more requirements on the web browser. As the technology is still evolving quickly, recent web browsers should be used with rich web clients. On the one hand, it's good for standardization purposes that corporations usually have the same browser installed on all workstations; however, this may be an older version that does not work well with rich web clients. For example, Internet Explorer 6 can still be found in many corporations as the default browser, which does not work very well with rich web clients. The main reason for this is that companies often still use early rich web clients with special ActiveX functionality that made the applications work in Internet Explorer 6. Upgrading to Internet Explorer 7 would be beneficial for many new rich web clients, but in some cases it would make the existing rich web clients work incorrectly. This is a big issue, as existing applications usually have higher priorities than new applications, and it makes the total cost of deploying new applications higher than expected.

Because JavaScript is employed in rich web clients slightly beyond its original intentions, it is not a very stable runtime environment. For business-critical applications that are used throughout an entire working day, this could be an issue, as a browser crash could cause a user to lose some of his work. However, browser manufacturers are working to make JavaScript execution more robust and fix memory leaks.

When compared to non-rich web applications, the additional interaction allows, for example, self-maintenance of personal data for phone books, or for multiple members of a department to contribute to its knowledge base. These applications are usually the same as before, but enriched with user management and some interaction. Full-size applications, however, still mostly remain in the rich client world, outside the browser.

History Is Repeating Itself

While this chapter gives a description of rich clients, web clients, and rich web clients, this leaves a question open: "Is there something like a non-rich version of a rich client?"

In fact, there is one (or better, there *was* one—it has nearly died out, but it still exists in large companies, especially in the finance sector). These are called *terminal applications*, and they run on *host computers*. These applications can be considered as representatives of the traditional client application type, but their characteristics are surprisingly similar to web clients. Users have to use a terminal program instead of a browser to connect to the host. Application logic is completely on the server, and the terminals just render the forms to input and read data.

The move from terminal application toward rich clients involved new programming languages, new hardware platforms, and increased input and output capabilities. In the realm of web development, the evolution was somewhat slower, but still involved a mental shift as well. Logic was moved from the server to the client, allowing more interaction on the client side without server roundtrips.

The mouse as an input device also played a big role in the evolution of applications. By using the mouse, users were able to manipulate and use screen elements that were nontextual. While software for things like accounting and text processing works without this feature, software for media editing does not. While it was not possible to do picture editing with host applications, it became so with rich clients. The very same evolution is happening today: until now, it was considered impossible to do picture editing in a web application, because this would basically have meant many roundtrips to the server on each operation. However, some online photo-editing applications are already out there, using a mixture of server- and client-side editing functionality that is transparent for the user.

Interestingly, more terminal applications have been converted to web applications than to rich client applications, as the concept was the same and only the rendering technology had to be rewritten. Rich clients were mainly new creations that took advantage of the new possibilities.

Taking this technology evolution further down the road, we will have in the future rich client applications that run natively in the operating system, using the full capabilities of the computer. We will also have rich web clients that run inside a *web application platform*, which will be an evolution of the web browser that uses the full capabilities of HTML 5 and ECMAScript.

Having a look into the software industry today, there is a clear trend toward developing rich web clients that offer the same functionality as powerful rich clients. Many companies have stopped evolving web clients into rich web clients, but have restarted development from scratch, due the different philosophy used when developing rich web clients.

What to Choose Now?

The first important step in deciding whether to create your application with one of the aforementioned technologies is identifying whether you're actually creating an *application*.

For example, web sites, which are responsible for displaying static or dynamic content and let users to some extent contribute to it, have to adhere to a very specific design, either to conform to a corporate design or based on concepts from design agencies. A toolkit for creating uniform "rich client–style" applications is not very suitable for creating such web sites. While toolkits like Eclipse RAP can be used for developing web sites, their intended use is for developing applications, where functionality is the number one priority and a general common look and feel is requested, but no specific individual design. Additionally, applications allow a much greater interaction with the user than web sites. User contribution to Web 2.0 sites should not be confused with user interaction, as the first is about providing content in a form, and the other is about manipulating data and application controls to complete a workflow or solve a business task.

For this book, the working assumption is that you'll be creating applications, not web sites.

When comparing rich clients to rich web clients, it looks as though rich clients will always be a bit ahead, as operating system features can be directly accessed, while rich web clients have to wait for web standards to appear and to be implemented by browser manufacturers. They also may have to wait for tool vendors to support particular functionalities, or invent custom solutions based on certain browser plug-ins.

On the other hand, browsers do offer a nice operating system abstraction level, which can be very useful for managing applications in a heterogeneous hardware environment, as long as the application requirements do not exceed what HTML and JavaScript are capable of doing.

To decide what to build, do a quick check of the key criteria:

- Is complete offline functionality required (e.g., for salespeople who work at a customer site where there might be no network connection)?

  If yes, then you should build a rich client application.

- Are many local files involved in the workflow handled by the application, and do those files have to remain local?

  If yes, then you should build a rich client application.

- Is the application intended mostly for reading, but not editing textual data?

  If yes, then you should build a web client application.

- Is easy management of applications that have fairly complex features required?

  If yes, then you should build a rich web client application.

In the end, the decision is often based on personal preferences. When there is no clear advantage of the one or the other technology, availability of developers, documentation, and taste may play a part in the decision-making progress.

Perhaps Eclipse RAP is an even better choice, as it tries to deal with this standoff between technologies, as outlined in Chapter 2.

Later, in Chapter 4, you use Eclipse RAP to build a rich web client application that you will also be able to launch as a rich client application. This will ease the decision process by removing the need to decide on a platform early on.

In Chapter 5,you will see how to convert an already existing Eclipse Rich Client Platform (RCP) application into a rich web client application using Eclipse RAP.

Chapter 2: Introducing Eclipse RAP

This chapter covers the main aspects of Eclipse RAP, focusing largely on abstract concepts rather than technical details, which is important early in the technology decision-making process. I'll dig deeper into the technical details of Eclipse RAP in Chapter 3.

The RAP Vision

Eclipse Rich Ajax Platform (RAP) empowers developers to build rich web clients "the Eclipse way." This can be separated into multiple goals:

- Allowing componentized, event-driven web application design
- Supporting web application programming using Java APIs
- Developing web applications like Java SWT applications
- Bringing the Eclipse Rich Client Platform (RCP) to the Web
- Customizing web applications using plug-ins
- Evolving RCP applications with great code reuse

This chapter will go over these goals, describe design goals, and discuss why certain choices have been made.

Componentized and Event-Driven Design

A fundamental concept of Java is reusable components. Components have some controller and view logic, and just need a model plugged in to do their job. The idea behind components is that they can be easily reused and developers can concentrate on business logic, rather than on fiddling around with presentation and basic manipulation. They also facilitate a consistent look and feel throughout an entire application. As a nice bonus, components and their reuse can save development money.

Components can communicate by listening to and sending events, which make communication between components convenient. Events allow for more flexible coding, as not all components have to know each other. Listeners can be seen as an early form of dependency injection.

While implementations like JSF are component-driven, there is still a lack of frameworks that integrate events in an easy way. Some web frameworks are beginning to support events, but most still rely on the traditional form submit or page request flow, where developers then have to read values from requests and do a lot of low-level coding on their own, rather than just using component and event APIs. Eclipse RAP heavily uses component models for development, and it also allows the creation of custom components according well-defined APIs.

Programming Using Java APIs

Besides having componentized architecture, the most important design goal of Eclipse RAP was to eliminate the need to develop in something other than Java. There are many Java developers who are capable of developing rich usable applications for businesses; however, they would have to be trained in HTML and JavaScript to start developing web applications for businesses. Also, nowadays it is much easier to recruit skilled Java enterprise or RCP developers than seasoned JavaScript developers.

The ability to create web applications in Java should not be underestimated. Integration between the web application and the Java back-end is very hard to achieve with non-Java languages. This drawback often cannot be compensated for by the possibly better abilities of non-Java frameworks (like Ruby on Rails, symfony, or Django) to create nice rich web clients.

Also, by using a Java API, RAP makes use of the great existing Java tooling. With RAP, developers can run quick JUnit tests against the code, rather than to trying to work with the comparably slow HtmlUnit or Selenium to figure out how something is rendered and interacted with in a browser. Java IDEs have full debugging and refactoring support. When multiple different languages or technologies are involved, developers need to manually change some Java, JSP, and JavaScript with three different tools, requiring them to find the relevant code pieces by hand, because there is no tool support. In pure Java that is not required, as IDEs can assist with finding the code pieces, changing and testing them.

That using Java APIs is a good idea is also proven by the fact that this concept is also adapted more or less by other frameworks. For example, Google Web Toolkit, Wicket, and Tapestry also use a Java API to model components and concepts to some extent. But they all basically still use HTML as the design language for what is being displayed, and require some JavaScript wrangling to get everything working as intended. There is no need for that in RAP, as everything has a known presentation delivered by the framework, very much like Swing Widget Toolkit (SWT).

Developing for the Web Just As with Java SWT

Taking the previous point further, there are already some very good and proven Java APIs for developing user interfaces:

- Swing, which evolved from the Abstract Window Toolkit (AWT)
- SWT, which was created as part of Eclipse

As a brief comparison, Swing contains its own visual representation, and SWT relies on the operating system for rendering. Both have their pros and cons, but as RAP is an Eclipse project and was designed for integration with RCP and the operating system, it reimplements SWT. That means that if developers are able to develop SWT applications, they can without any further training develop RAP applications. RAP encapsulates Ajax technologies into simple-to-use Java components the same way SWT encapsulates native widgets. The SWT API has been optimized to develop rich client business applications, which is an additional advantage.

These factors provide distinct advantages over new proprietary APIs like Google Web Toolkit and Wicket, which would have to be learned and understood by the developers. Using the proven and widely known SWT API makes Eclipse RAP an extremely handy toolkit.

Bringing Eclipse RCP to the Web

Eclipse RCP is a very powerful framework. Besides user interface components, it provides many utility services, like the Workbench, layout managers, online help support, a preference store, and a security model.

Evolved from a platform intended to power the Eclipse IDE, RCP became a platform supporting the functionality requirements of business applications. So it seems natural to bring these features into rich web clients intended for business applications. However, the whole platform is a very large chunk, and powerful JavaScript clients would be required to deal with its functionality.

Eclipse RAP solves this issue by separating RCP into a server and a client application, where the client is just the screen on the browser and RCP runs on the server, preventing the JavaScript clients from doing the heavy lifting in business logic. This makes it possible to bring all the features of RCP, even the more complex ones, to the Web.

One of Eclipse RCP's key concepts is that it supports, or actually is composed of, plug-ins. Most of the core services are plug-ins, and custom code can be easily added with plug-ins. (Of course, it would be great to have this in RAP web applications as well.)

Customizing Web Applications with Plug-ins

Plug-ins allow very easy extension of functionality with source code provided by third parties. The good integration makes installation of plug-ins as easy as dropping them into the `eclipse/plugins` folder.

Plug-ins don't just enable integrating third-party components, but also allow better decoupled distributed application development and company-wide code reuse. They also support maintenance of live software, because plug-ins are easy to upgrade. As long as a plug-in is not currently in use, it can even be exchanged while an application is running.

Plug-ins can automatically hook into predefined slots, called *extension points*, and are active without further configuration.

Plug-ins can be used to support customization. For example, perhaps only administrators will get an administrator plug-in, or two plug-ins might deliver two different look-and-feel assets, and the correct plug-in will be chosen based on the locale of the user.

As Eclipse RAP is totally based on the Eclipse plug-in mechanism, this comes for free. There's no need to custom-code a plug-in registry, deal with hot deployment of plug-ins, or invent an extension point concept. It is all there.

Evolving RCP Applications Through Code Reuse

As there are plenty of RCP applications out in the wild, it would be wasted effort to rewrite them just to make them available on the Web.

Eclipse RAP tries to bring those applications to the Web with as much code reuse as possible. Although there are many technical challenges to overcome to achieve this, RAP has managed to make it possible with very little effort on the developer side. Chapter 3 will explain how RAP uses the SWT API to make it basically transparent to the developer, whether he develops with SWT or RAP. As a result, there is no real need to change existing code, because this should be hidden from the application.

There are a few points that should be considered when designing an RCP application that should also use RAP, which will be described in Chapter 5.

But the general promise is still valid: Eclipse RAP enables existing RCP application to be used on the Web, while also allowing the creation of web applications that run on the desktop.

RAP Case Studies

In this section, five different scenarios are described. The first two are pretty generic, the third proposes a RAP implementation of an existing RCP application, and the remaining two feature two existing products based on Eclipse RAP.

Scenario 1: Freedom of Choice

As mentioned in Chapter 1, it can be a matter of taste whether a certain application should be an RCP or a RAP application. Sometimes no decision in favor of one can be made, or it should be checked in a proof-of-concept project whether one or the other works out better. This is especially true for longer development projects, where it is unknown whether rich clients or rich web clients will be the favored solution at the time of release.

For these cases, RAP leaves both paths open, as no wrong decision can be made when doing a RAP-compatible implementation.

Scenario 2: Business-to-Customer Solutions

In this scenario, imagine a corporation considering opening up an internal application for end customers via the Internet for self-service use. Such an application could be modular, and the modules that will be accessible for customer could be exposed using Eclipse RAP. This allows code reuse for internal and external functionality. Customers could use the RAP application to maintain their data, and access, for example, their orders, while the internal application could contain the same modules with some additional management modules. Either an RCP or a RAP application can be used internally.

Scenario 3: Intranet Productivity Tools

This scenario describes a complex RCP application and talks about further development options for it. The application is Lotus Notes, which is a calendar, e-mail, and contact-management application. Starting from version 8, it is implemented using Eclipse RCP. The screenshot in Figure 2-1 shows some of the complex features of this application.

Figure 2-1. IBM Lotus Notes

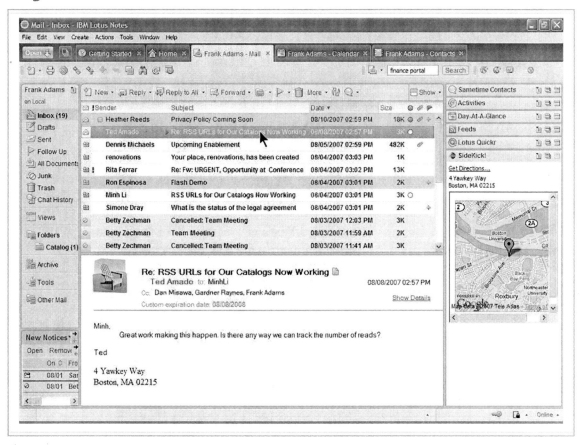

IBM migrated its Lotus Notes to be based on RCP to enable cross-platform usage of the application in Windows and Linux. It was a strategic decision to strengthen the support for Linux as a desktop operating system, enabling the user to choose the operating system more freely while keeping the application.

A possible next step on this path would be to use RAP for transforming Lotus Notes into a web application for worldwide access to e-mail and more. In the current version, IBM reimplemented the web part of Lotus Notes from scratch, as did Microsoft with Outlook Web Access; however, both products suffer in many areas of functionality.

Eclipse RAP could have given IBM a neat, cheap web solution for Lotus Notes. Depending on the SWT and JFace APIs used by Lotus Notes, this could have been achieved with a large amount of code reuse, saving development and maintenance costs. More details on Lotus Notes can be found at www.ibm.com/software/lotus/products/notes.

The value in providing RCP applications as RAP versions in the corporate intranet is worldwide accessibility.

Data should be stored on the server anyway, so it is not uncommon to make the application dealing with the data available on the server.

Note   Generally, it is easy to migrate an existing RCP application to RAP. The procedure for that is described in Chapter 5. You might need to slightly redesign certain pieces of code, but this will be limited.

Scenario 4: End Customer Solutions

Yoxos On Demand is an application developed by Innopract using RAP. It allows customers to customize their own Eclipse download bundle. The main view of Yoxos is shown in Figure 2-2.

Figure 2-2. Yoxos On Demand

The bundle contains user-selected and compatibility-checked third-party plug-ins and Eclipse projects. It comes with a set of preconfigured bundles for different use cases. Users can use this application remotely on the server, without any additional software required.

By using RAP, Innopract has been able to use plug-ins, manage installation easily, and let Eclipse users configure their Eclipse download in a familiar Eclipse-like user interface. Yoxos On Demand was the first proof-of-concept application implemented with RAP.

More details on Yoxos can be found at `http://ondemand.yoxos.com/geteclipse/start`.

The value in proving a web user interface using Eclipse RAP is twofold. For RCP developers, it is much easier to achieve than using any other framework. It also is much simpler to implement due to the availability of a wide variety of standard components. It is more convenient to deal with more session state than in other frameworks.

For the end user, the application feels more powerful. This is not to say that other rich web clients are not powerful, but that Eclipse RAP applications are easier to grasp for the user. There is no risk of losing context while navigating through multiple pages; a whole workflow can be done on one screen. As RAP applications give the choice of using a native theme, users can also apply known concepts and use the application more efficiently.

Tip　　　Using themes, Eclipse RAP applications can look either like RCP clients or other Web 2.0 sites. Custom styling allows the designer to find the right balance between the two for the application. Chapter 4 contains some instructions on how to change the look and feel by playing around with the basic components (e.g. by making the main window not look like a window).

Scenario 5: Business Solutions As Services

PIA is a software-as-a-service customer relationship management application, built with Eclipse RAP technology by CAS Software AG. A contact editor for PIA is shown in Figure 2-3.

Figure 2-3. CAS PIA contact editor

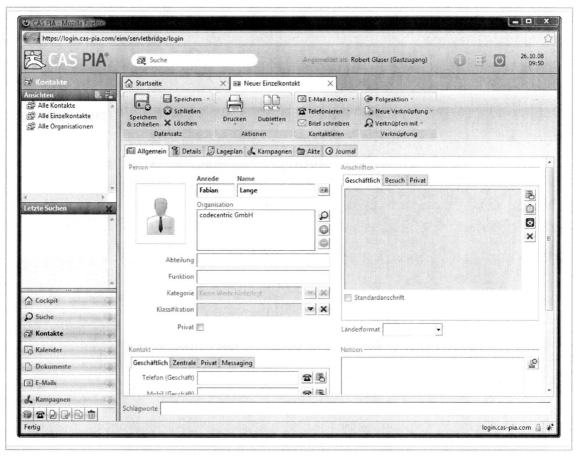

CAS has created PIA as software that can be used by customers as a service. Plug-ins can be created to perform customer-specific customizations easily on existing applications without any need to change the main code base, enabling perfect reselling of the same core functionality without crippling the ability to customize.

The software is hosted and managed by the service provider, enabling customers to just buy time/user licenses without any installation or maintenance. And as bonus, the application is available everywhere.

The application offers the same functionality as other comparable rich client customer relationship management applications. With any other technology besides RAP, it would have been very hard for CAS to deliver competitive functionality in its web application.

Eclipse RAP allows either an evolution of existing RCP code to a web service solution, or the creation of a web service solution that can be shipped as a rich client to customers. Eclipse RAP opens up new possibilities for new businesses without closing down existing offerings.

More details on PIA and a demo login can be found at `www.cas-pia.de`.

Pitfalls with RAP

While RAP might look like a great solution so far, it isn't perfect. There are some areas where RAP can make trouble, so it's good to be prepared. Luckily, the RAP development team is aware of these areas, and the next version may already fix some of the issues. Chapter 3 will contain some details about current and old versions of RAP.

Wrong Expectations

There are some usability issues with rich web clients, due to the fact that users can have wrong expectations based on the visual impression. For example, users usually associate appearance with certain behavior, and vice versa. Here are some examples:

- In the earlier days of the Internet, users were used to clicking only on links, not images. Two factors helped users to identify links:

    - Links were blue

    - Links were underlined

    Today, design agencies have managed to remove the underlining, as it disturbs a nice clean design, but very often the link is still blue. Additionally, links often react on mouseover—for example, by displaying an underline to confirm to the user that it is really a link.

    This psychological effect can be easily tested with a colleague, friend, or family member. Create a web page, style two or three words in blue, and underline them. You can be pretty sure that nearly everybody will hover over those words and try to click them.

- If the active window looks like a text editor, containing mainly a large text area with just some supporting toolbars, users will expect the application to behave like most editors behave.

    The most common expectation will be that you can press Ctrl+S to save the document. But with many web mail clients, for example, the draft will not be saved. Instead, the browser will open a dialog and prompt the user to save the HTML. Google Mail learned this and supports saving using this keyboard shortcut, making it much more convenient to use.

There are even more subtle differences to keyboard shortcuts. Programmatically waiting for Ctrl+S with JavaScript will not work on Macs, where users are used to Apple+S.

- If there are multiple input fields on a page, users expect to be able to use the Tab key to navigate between them. Besides this being expected behavior, it is also good usability. A common concern when switching from a rich client application to a web client application is that such simple and powerful functionality is often not preserved. Many badly designed web applications prove this.

- If there are smaller windows with a window title bar, people expect to be able to double-click the title bar to maximize the windows. Eclipse RAP supports this feature out of the box.

- If elements like picture thumbnails in a gallery are shown, people expect to be able to either drag and drop or copy and paste to reorder them. This pitfall is also known as the *explorer anti-pattern*. Sometimes items are displayed like they are in a native explorer, but the functionality is different. This greatly confuses users and should be avoided.

The closer a rich web client comes to the look and feel of a rich client application (or any other frequently used application), the more users will expect similar behavior. This is characterized as a downside here, but ultimately can be an advantage, as mentioned in Chapter 1. Users do not have to learn the application; they intuitively understand how to use it from previous learning.

In fact, RAP deals pretty well with these issues. As an additional tool, RAP supports themes, which can completely change the look and feel of applications to emphasize certain usage concepts. Themes are discussed in Chapter 6.

Lower Performance

As with performance it is pretty much as with wrong expectations. On one hand, users expect web applications to be slower than rich client applications. However, users of rich web applications that look like rich client applications have higher expectations with respect to performance than users of traditional web clients.

Having a short look at the technical facts, RAP applications have lots of JavaScript code involved on the client side, and nearly every action by the user will result in an Ajax request replicating state information to the server or requesting new data. To cope with this issue, some mouse and keyboard events are not supported by RAP, resulting in better performance with slight functionality reduction.

Interestingly, there is an order of magnitude difference in browser performance. All the latest major browsers work fast enough, except Internet Explorer. Version 7 is really slow, and even the latest betas of Internet Explorer 8 are still way behind the others.

Also, keep in mind that running an applications multiple times on the server is not the way Java is intended to scale. When greater scalability is required, the business logic should be moved to traditional Java enterprise concepts (distributed Enterprise Java Beans [EJBs]), and RAP should be left for the user interface part, resulting in a three-tier architecture with RAP taking the middle-tier role, rather than a two-tier client-server model.

Still, RAP applications have great performance, and the developers are still making improvements. For example, RAP 1.2 will include a good JavaScript compression engine enabled by default.

At the same time, users can be irritated by the application performance and say that the application feels more sluggish than a real rich client does. Ideally, the application will uses established techniques like progress bars or other types of wait indicators to help users understand the delays.

No Web in Web

While the RAP model allows developers to avoid writing HTML or JavaScript, when it comes to integrating third-party web applications, these may again be required. RAP has some support for this, by allowing the use of a browser widget, which is basically an IFrame that is controlled by the application. However, the communication between the RAP application and the third-party web application displayed inside the browser widget is limited, due to browser security restrictions. A second option is writing a custom JavaScript widget to integrate third-party JavaScript. Chapter 6 describes all steps required to develop and include such a widget.

However, especially with other JavaScript-heavy applications, you should avoid mashing them up with RAP. RAP works best when it would work the same in RCP, but web mashups won't work in RCP, unless you take the extra work of developing a RAP widget, which then includes or combines those mashups. However, this would be more of a programmed mashup, rather than a user-created one. Perhaps it can be seen as a drawback that Eclipse RAP uses too much Java and too little HTML for web applications, but perhaps it is just a question of mindset when approaching the development of an RCP and rich web client application with RAP.

It is good practice to run your application in the respective other environment from time to time to see if it works from a look-and-feel or usability point of view, and to be reminded of the dual-environment functionality that RAP supports. However, it is unlikely that it will not work in the RCP environment when it can compile in RAP. Chapter 5 will elaborate this concept more in detail.

Chapter 3: The RAP Architecture

This chapter describes the technical architecture of Eclipse RAP. It compares the RAP stack with the stack used by RCP and highlights the differences and commonalities. In a nutshell: *RAP has replaced most RCP interfaces with its own implementation.*

Figure 3-1 gives a possible presentation of the components involved in the RCP and RAP stacks. They will each be explained and compared throughout the chapter. Notice in the figure that the top levels are identical and only the lower levels have been changed by the RAP team.

Figure 3-1. RCP and RAP architecture compared

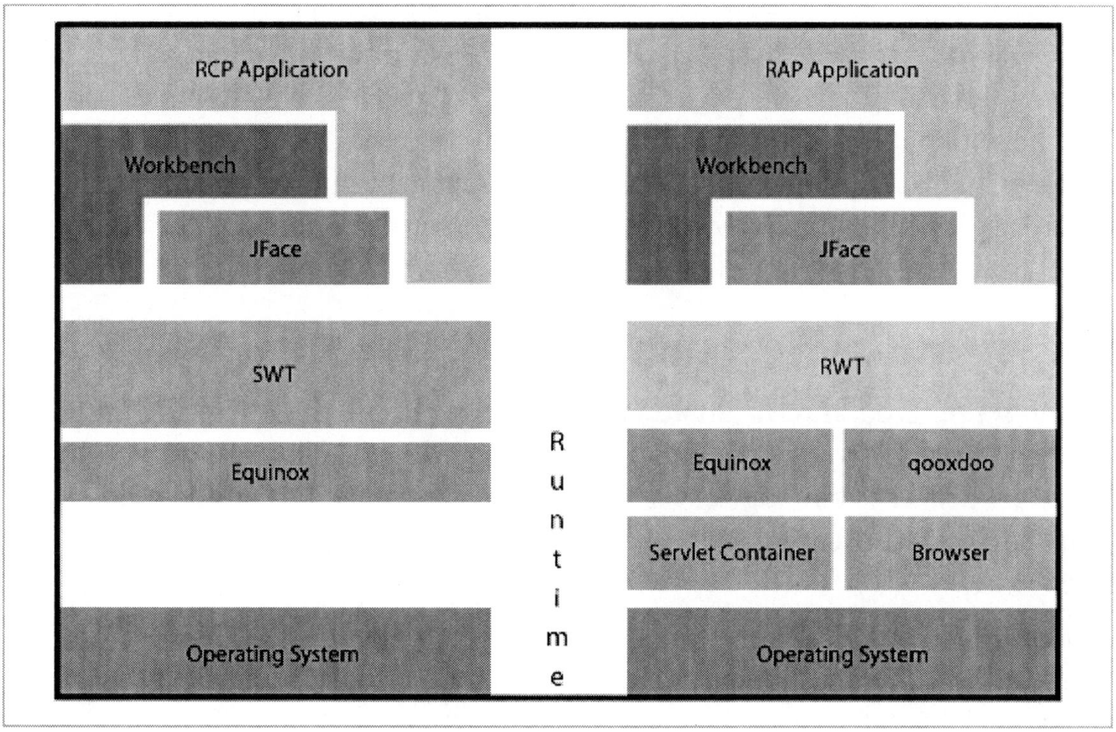

The Runtime Layer

In the RCP case, the runtime layer is pretty simple. It is composed of the host operating system and a standard Java Runtime Edition VM, on which sits an OSGi implementation that is used by the Workbench to provide the plug-in service. *OSGi*, specified in JSR-291, specifies how different modules, or plug-ins (called *bundles* in OSGi terms), can expose their services.

Above OSGi is SWT, which does not use OSGi but is drawn above it, because it contains components and is not just an infrastructure level like OSGi. SWT uses functionality provided through the JVM from the operating system to render the native widgets.

For RAP, there are two existing runtimes. One resides on the server side, powering the main RAP stack, and the other resides on the client side, running the user interface part. One design goal of RAP was to make sure that the application-facing interfaces are the same, so that it wouldn't matter which stack the applications run on. As such, the server-side stack of RAP, where the application is running, is almost the same as the RCP one.

The Server Side

On the server side in RAP, there is a JVM as well, but the operating system does not need to provide means for rendering widgets. This allows you to use a real server to run the server side, as it doesn't need to understand visuals. Often, this type of server is called *headless*. This JVM runs two platforms:

One is also an OSGi implementation, which is Equinox in the Eclipse case. As in the RCP case, Equinox is responsible for dependency management of the modules and enables hot deployment of new versions or extensions. RAP takes advantage of the fact that RCP uses Equinox as well to power the plug-in concept in Eclipse. Certain RCP bundles are simply replaced by RAP ones; others are reused as they are.

The other platform is a servlet container, responsible for doing the typical web stuff: handling requests. This could be a Tomcat or Jetty server, or even a heavier one like WebLogic or WebSphere. However, there is no need for any server-specific functionality, as the server is only used for communication with the client web browser. The requests are picked up by a servlet bridge and handed to the Equinox system.

Interestingly, it does not matter if the servlet container is launched from Equinox, which is usually the case in development environments, or if the web archive that is deployed to a servlet container contains the Equinox runtime, as in many production environments. The bonus of this is that a RAP application can be treated like any other web application from an administrator's point of view.

In both scenarios, the application developed with RAP is provided as OSGi bundles that sit alongside the RAP core bundles in the Equinox runtime. Both deployment scenarios are covered in Chapter 7. When run, there is just one instance of RAP and the application, rather than multiple instances of the application stack, which is especially common in scripting languages.

The Client Side

On the client side, there is the client operating system, where the browser runs. There are no restrictions on the operating system, but there are some on the browser. The browser acts like a JVM, providing some standard services to the upper layers (most notably a JavaScript engine, which the browser has to support). Unfortunately, the different browser vendors still implement the JavaScript interpreter in a nonstandard way; this requires either an additional abstraction layer or a lot of additional cross-browser JavaScript code from the RAP team.

Instead of coding the majority of the JavaScript code from scratch, the RAP team chose one of the many available JavaScript libraries to power the client side. The choice was made to use qooxdoo as the user interface part on the client side as part of the RAP bundle. qooxdoo provides a JavaScript framework for solving cross-browser issues as well as for rendering user interfaces with complete widgets and communicating with them. In fact, qooxdoo allows JavaScript widgets to be treated almost the same as SWT widgets, which is a perfect fit for RAP. There is a small amount of RAP-specific JavaScript code on the client side to bootstrap RAP and adapt the qooxdoo interfaces to the RAP/RCP ones. From another point of view, it could be said that only Java-to-JavaScript translation is required from the RAP team to create and use widgets on the client side.

ABOUT QOOXDOO

qooxdoo (pronounced *COOKS-doo*) is an open source JavaScript framework created by the German company 1&1 Internet. It provides basic JavaScript framework code for cross-browser functionality and Ajax, like any other JavaScript framework, but additionally comes with a remarkable GUI library that allows the creation of rich web clients without any HTML or CSS knowledge. Its component model is closely related to the Swing and SWT component models, which makes it suitable for Java developers to work with. qooxdoo is dual licensed under the LGPL and EPL licenses.

You can find more information on qooxdoo at www.qooxdoo.org.

Note   As additional advice, it is always beneficial to use a JavaScript library when hand-writing Java Script code. A library makes code more robust, easier to write, and better to maintain. Some examples of other first-class libraries are jQuery, Prototype, MooTools, Dojo, and YUI.

Reimplemented APIs

The main task of RAP is to provide reimplementations of three big subframeworks: SWT, Workbench, and JFace. The RAP approach for reimplementation was to take the complete original code, move it over to the RAP plug-ins, and edit everything that didn't work in RAP.

You can see this easily by checking the RAP source code. To allow you to find the RAP modifications in the original implementation, the RAP team used a special pattern to tag their modifications, as follows:

```
// RAP [developer]: comment
// original code
   new code
// RAPEND: [developer]
```

Here's an example of a font size calculation change in the JFace dialog:

```
// RAP [bm]: GC
// int l = gc.textExtent(s).x;
   int l = Graphics.textExtent(getFont(), s, 0).x;
// RAPEND: [bm]
```

The number of changes required for RAP in version 1.1.1 was 2,090 (assuming that every code piece was correctly tagged). Future versions of RAP will bring these numbers down by implementing APIs that did not exist before. Also, future versions of the Workbench, SWT, and JFace APIs will help reduce these numbers by improving their implementation to be more RAP-friendly.

Standard Widget Toolkit

The SWT API from the RPC side was reimplemented by RAP under the name RAP Widget Toolkit (RWT). Instead of drawing to the GraphicalContext, the object communicating with the screen buffer of the operating system, RWT creates the required JavaScript commands that cause qooxdoo to render the appropriate widgets. These commands are compressed and sent to the browser using Ajax. To make this happen timely, the client will always have an Ajax request open that can be used for delivering some user interface updates to the client. Commands coming in while a request is being returned are collected until the new request comes in from the client, and are then sent in one batch. Perhaps in the future, when web socket protocols have matured and become widely supported, this can be replaced with support a server-push model rather than the current tweaked client-pull model (also known as Comet).

JFace

JFace is an addition to SWT, designed to create a friendlier API for developers who did not really like SWT. It provides some more complete ready-made components, called viewers, and additional utilities, like useful convenience APIs, field validation, dialogs, and an action concept. Its *virtual viewers* are essential tools when it comes to displaying large amounts of data, as they support lazy loading. Its functionality blurs slightly into the Workbench, as it in fact uses some Workbench code.

RAP maps most of the JFace API; in fact, most recent additions to RAP have been made with regard to JFace, as it is used very frequently by developers. Unlike the Workbench code, JFace required more recoding from the RAP team, as both the SWT and Workbench APIs were incomplete. And as the JFace API is also very large and powerful, there are still areas that are just not implemented by RAP (e.g., the ability to custom-style components as the StyledText class or create complex drawings with HTML elements).

The Workbench

The Workbench provides the communication infrastructure with components like activities, commands, and context. Additionally, it allows the notion of hierarchical and logical grouping of user interface components.

The hierarchy goes like this: Window contains Menu/Toolbar and Page, which are managed by a perspective. The Page can contain different views and an editor, which is a special-purpose view.

If there is a central component in RCP, it is the Workbench. The main issue with the RCP Workbench model from a RAP perspective is that, due to historical reasons, the Workbench assumes that only one user is capable of using it. For example, objects holding user state were implemented as singletons. This limitation left two options for the RAP team:

- Creating a Workbench for every remote user
- Rewriting Workbench code so that it can handle multiple users

The RAP team chose the latter, because the memory consumption for a new Workbench for every user would just be too much. Also, the latter choice made the Workbench multiuser-capable. This required some work, but the RAP team is actually contributing modifications to the RCP Workbench team, enabling future versions of the Workbench to run multiple users in RCP and reducing the memory footprint for the RAP use case. Some implications of this multiuser modification for the Workbench are described in the following section.

Issues and Solutions

While RAP is a great solution for many cases and its architecture is very interesting, the complexity involved in the RAP technology creates some limitations. Chapter 5 will describe patterns for dealing with these issues. This section will outline some of them, along with their implications and possible solutions, as well as the direction the future development of Eclipse RAP will go to resolve the issues.

RAP Does Not Implement All APIs Yet

RAP currently provides a subset of most RCP APIs. Among the missing ones are some optional Workbench stuff, some JFace APIs, and a few events, plus some other stuff that most likely will never be implemented, just because nobody is using or requesting support for it. As the most important and commonly used APIs are implemented, this is not a big issue; however, every project will find an RCP API that doesn't (yet) exist. In such cases, there are three options:

- Try not use that particular API.
- Create a workaround—for example, using patch fragments.
- Implement a clean solution and submit it to the RAP sandbox.

While the first option is of course possible, the RAP team will happily accept the third option, as the unimplemented APIs mainly result from time restrictions, and are not the result of impracticality. The RAP sandbox was especially designed for user contributions of missing APIs. For infrequent contributions, sending implementations to the RAP bug tracker or the developer mailing list could also be an option. As with any open source project, RAP lives from contributions and improvements from the community, so you should always consider contributing.

RAP Will Never Implement Certain APIs

Unfortunately, some APIs are missing because of architectural differences between a native and a browser application, or because they would cause severe performance issues.

For example, there is no `GraphicalContext` class (`org.eclipse.swt.graphics.GC`), as you simply cannot paint on the screen freely in a web application. Some other functionality of `GC`, like finding out text size, is available from the `Graphics` class as a static helper rather than instance method. For example, instead of `aGCInstance.stringExtent(String string)`, you invoke `Graphics.stringExtent(Font font, String string)`.

NEVER SAY NEVER AGAIN

The current assumption of the RAP team is that they will never create a mapping for GC; however, more and more JavaScript developers are discovering the `canvas` tag, which is defined in the HTML 5 specification and is already implemented in Safari, Firefox, and Opera browsers. The `canvas` element actually allows painting on it, like the GC does for RCP. So perhaps future versions of RAP could support that.

Resource objects will have no `dispose()` method. The reason for this is that resources should not be created and disposed per user, but should be obtained via factories provided by JFace that will supply the singleton instance of that resource to multiple clients. When doing so, it would not make sense for one client to invoke the `dispose()` method of a resource that another client is using. Also, resources in the web context are not byte arrays in the heap as they would be in RCP; in RAP, they just reference a URL that will be loaded by the browser when using this resource. By using this approach, memory consumption is greatly reduced.

RAP is Multiuser

For traditional web frameworks, the idea of an application being accessed by multiple users at the same time is nothing new. But RCP was never intended to be run by multiple users, so RAP had to deal with that by creating a multiuser layer inside the platform. Because developers can also implement code that is possibly conflicting when it is accessed by multiple users, they have to be reminded that their application needs to be multiuser-safe. Handling multiple users not only means more consumed memory for storing application state, but that objects from the Workbench that were considered singletons in the RCP case are no longer real singletons. For example, objects that store user-specific information are impacted by this.

RAP solves this by introducing the concept of `SessionSingletons`. These are unique for each user, and can be used by developers like this:

```
public class MySingleton extends SessionSingletonBase {
    public static MySingleton getInstance() {
        return (MySingleton)getInstance(MySingleton.class);
    }
    // all the other stuff comes here
}
```

Some other singletons are globally unique and can be used by all users simultaneously. A similar example is the internationalization (I18N) feature, where in the RCP case, the language can be determined on startup and stored in a singleton. In a multiuser environment, there must be one instance of the resource bundle per session, or the browsers can switch languages while the application is running.

For memory consumption, it is even more important to implement carefully. RAP makes reuse of resources possible, but the developer has to keep in mind that there will be multiple users on one server. For that, it is a good idea to use the virtual viewer components from JFace that load only the displayed data on demand.

With respect to scalability, the RAP team has tested servers that can handle roughly 250 users per GB RAM and CPU core. The nature of RAP running on a central server allows you to place business logic outside of the RAP container and access it remotely—for example, via EJBs. This will turn the RAP server into a presentation host and create a service layer that is accessible not only from RAP applications but also from other applications. It additionally allows smooth scaling of the components that cause heavy load.

RAP Plug-ins and Packages

The RAP version control system includes the sandbox and runtime folders. The sandbox folder contains mostly community contributions and experimental code, which is intended for user contributions, and might or might not be merged later into the official package. Inside the `runtime` folder are following plug-ins:

- `org.eclipse.rap.jface`
- `org.eclipse.rap.jface.databinding`
- `org.eclipse.rap.ui`
- `org.eclipse.rap.ui.forms`
- `org.eclipse.rap.ui.views`
- `org.eclipse.rap.ui.workbench`

These plug-ins reflect the structure of Eclipse RCP, which has the same plug-ins for RCP instead of RAP. The actual Java packages inside are identical, and have the same API.

The Eclipse project uses Concurrent Version System (CVS), and the RAP repository can be accessed from the following URL: `http://dev.eclipse.org/viewcvs/index.cgi/org.eclipse.rap/?root=Technology_Project`.

Or do a checkout from CVS using a `pserver` connection to `dev.eclipse.org:/cvsroot/technology`. The RAP project is located inside the folder `org.eclipse.rap`.

To ease the process of getting the projects from the CVS repository, there is a Team Project Set file available that can be used to automatically import the projects.

RAP Version History

This book covers Eclipse RAP 1.1.1. In general, the content is valid for older releases and the next 1.2 release as well, as the APIs and extension points are now identical to RCP, and the styling API is based on CSS, the standard for styling web apps. The main progress is now on making the API complete, rather than inventing new concepts.

The RAP team maintains its "New and Noteworthy" page at www.eclipse.org/rap/noteworthy.

The following list gives a brief overview of the evolution of RAP.

June 2006: Eclipse RAP project approved: Innopract contributed the initial code base from its World Wide Web Windowing Toolkit (W4T).

October 2007: 1.0 release: For the 1.0 release, RAP underwent massive API refactoring. From the original RAP APIs, everything was moved into the original RCP namespace. This greatly emphasized that RAP was intended to be a different rendering layer, rather than a different API. Table and tree widgets were the first that were close to par with their RCP relatives.

June 2008: 1.1 release: This release was part of the Eclipse Platform Ganymede release. Most important, it contains an implementation for `readAndDispatch()`, which works the same as in SWT. The Theming and Branding APIs were updated to use CSS instead of the previous proprietary format. Activities and image decorators became supported. Mouse click events were added, as well as the preference store.

September 2008: 1.1.1 service release: This release contains many bug fixes and is shipping the upgraded qooxdoo library in version 0.7.3.

June 2009: 1.2 release: This release will be part of the Eclipse Platform Galileo release. The main goals for 1.2 are RAP allowing multiple browser tabs and supporting the use of RAP applications in portlet environments. Already done are a date-picker implementation and an expand bar. Also, a new JavaScript compression reduces the initial payload by 20 percent.

The RAP Community

As RAP is still a very young project, it is important to know where more information can be found. RAP has a newsgroup where many of the core team members are active, at www.eclipse.org/newsportal/thread.php?group=eclipse.technology.rap.

Bugs or proposed tickets for Eclipse RAP are tracked in the Eclipse Bug Tracker, searchable from `https://bugs.eclipse.org/bugs/query.cgi?product=RAP`.

If you want to share widgets or contribute to the project in any way, you can obtain a user account with commit rights to the sandbox project from the RAP team.

Another recommended read is the RAP development team blog, which contains plenty of good information on very detailed topics, available at `http://rapblog.innoopract.com`.

An up-to-date list of recommended further reading, links to community mailing lists, and more are being compiled at the companion website for this book, at `www.rap-book.com`.

Chapter 4: Developing a RAP Application

The instructions in this book assume that you know how to use the Eclipse IDE and the navigators and editors, and especially that you can automatically import required packages (using Ctrl+O), as the code examples show only parts of classes and omit import declarations.

Additionally, RCP application knowledge is a good prerequisite; however, the instructions will be explicit enough for beginners as well. Code examples in this book use loose code style (e.g., variables are not declared as `final` and `@Override` annotations are not added) to keep them short. Class names are written in monospaced font (`like this`) and begin with an uppercase letter. Method names used in the text are followed by parentheses, like this: `methodName()`.

Live demos, code examples and errata are available for download from `www.rap-book.com/code`.

Installing the Eclipse and RAP SDKs

Note   The following instructions are valid for Eclipse 3.4 Ganymede, which is recommended and used throughout this book. For the examples, any 3.3.x or newer version is also very likely to work fine; please check `www.eclipse.org/rap/gettingstarted.php`. Also note that these instructions are tailored for Windows. However, they work the same on Linux or Mac OS X, just with different directories.

To get started with development, get the Eclipse for RCP/Plug-in Developers package from the Eclipse download site, at `www.eclipse.org/downloads`. Once the package is downloaded, extract it to `C:\RAP\`, where the extraction process will create a folder called `eclipse`. Start `eclipse.exe` from `C:\RAP\eclipse` and choose a workspace location; for example, `C:\RAP\ws`.

Once Eclipse is loaded, select Help ➤ Software Updates from the menu to install RAP. Switch to the Available Software tab and click the "Add Site" button. Enter the Eclipse RAP update site, `http://download.eclipse .org/technology/rap/update-site`, into the Location field of the dialog shown by Eclipse, and then click OK. By doing so, you will always get the latest stable RAP release.

This entry will now appear in the list. Check the box next to it, as shown in Figure 4-1, and click Install to download and install the Eclipse RAP SDK.

Figure 4-1. Choosing RAP on the Available Software tab

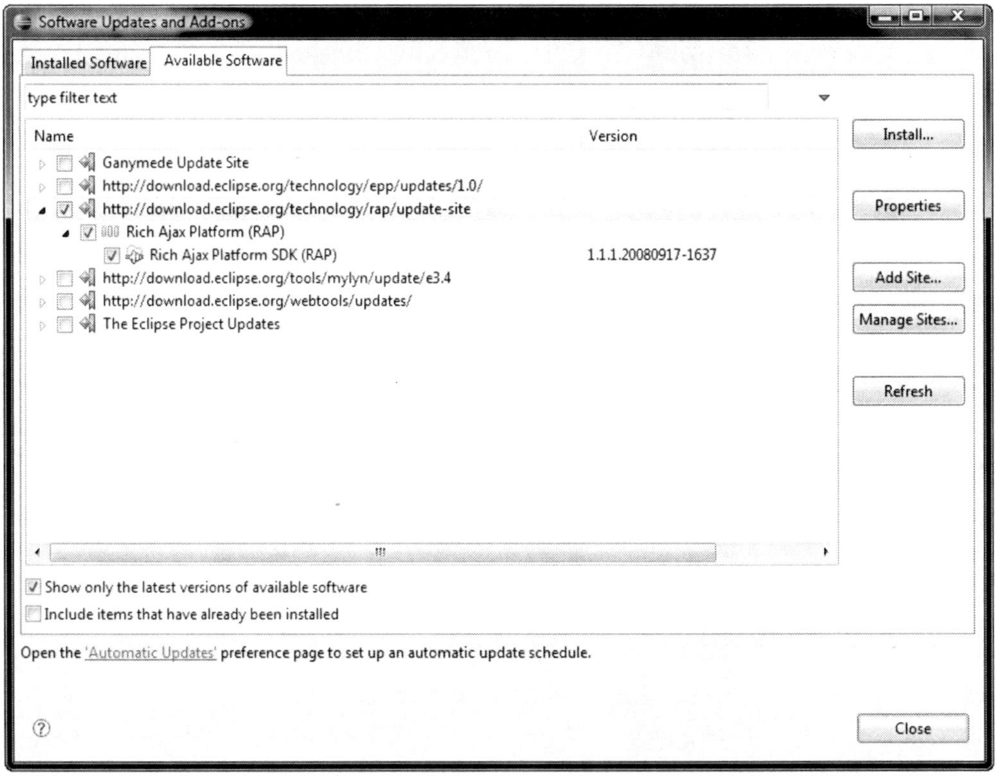

If you are using a different Eclipse package than the one with RCP, additional plug-ins will be added to the selection; otherwise, the wizard will just ask you to accept some licenses. Do so by clicking Next and then Finish.

The download will start. Once it has completed, Eclipse will prompt for restart. Confirm this by clicking Yes. Once Eclipse is restarted, the Overview screen will contain a new entry that reads "Rich Ajax Platform (RAP). Learn how to install and use the Rich Ajax Platform" (see Figure 4-2).

Figure 4-2. The Overview screen of the Eclipse RAP SDK

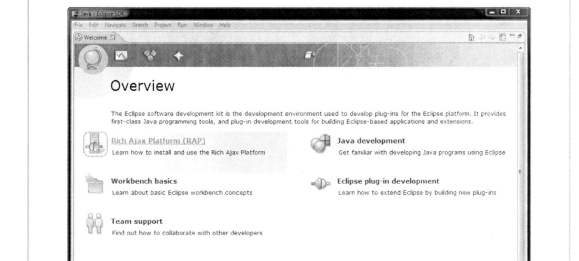

Select it and choose Install Target Platform. Choose C:\RAP\target from the displayed dialog and make sure that the check box labeled "Switch the target after installation" is checked. As the description says, this will reconfigure Eclipse to use a different platform for running applications. By default, this target platform is the same as the one running the development environment. For running RAP, it will not work using the development environment platform as a target, because some plug-ins of RAP and the IDE will conflict, because the IDE uses RCP code, which is not compatible with RAP.

This step will complete quite fast, because it just unpacks parts of the RAP SDK.

The default view of Eclipse 3.4 presented after launching Eclipse shows a task list view and a welcome view, which can be closed to free some screen real estate. You are free to configure the layout to your needs, but certain descriptions in this book will assume that you use the default layout. If you want to reset a perspective to its default settings, the Window ➤ Reset Perspective option takes care of this.

Open the Plug-in Development perspective from Window ➤ Open Perspective ➤ Other ➤ "Plug-in development," which will be the main perspective for developing RAP applications.

Running the RAP Sample Application

To run the RAP sample application, you first need to unpack it from the plug-in it is shipped with. Start with the Plug-in Development perspective and select the Plug-ins view on the left.

Right-click `org.eclipse.rap.demo` and select Import As ➤ Source Project, as shown in Figure 4-3.

Figure 4-3. Importing the sample application from the plug-in

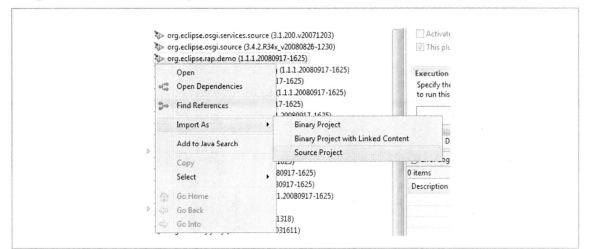

The source files of the demo plug-in will be extracted to a new project into the workspace. If you are interested in having a look at the other RAP source code, the same procedure can be applied to any other RAP or RCP plug-in, bringing them into the workspace. Additionally, Eclipse will prefer the workspace project over the embedded plug-in. This also allows for easier debugging or even changing some code inside plug-ins.

Switch back to the Package Explorer view and expand `org.eclipse` `.rap.demo`. After that, double-click the `plugin.xml` folder. The Overview screen, which is the main screen for editing the plug-in configuration, will appear, as shown in Figure 4-4.

Note   The same dialog can be also accessed by double-clicking `MANIFEST.MF` inside the `META-INF` directory. This is handy in some cases where `plugin.xml` is not yet generated. All changes to this configuration dialog can be also done with XML inside the `plugin.xml` file or in manifest style inside the `MANIFEST.MF` file. Feel free to check the generated code from the dialog by clicking the `plugin.xml` or `MANIFEST.MF` tab.

Figure 4-4. Launching the sample application

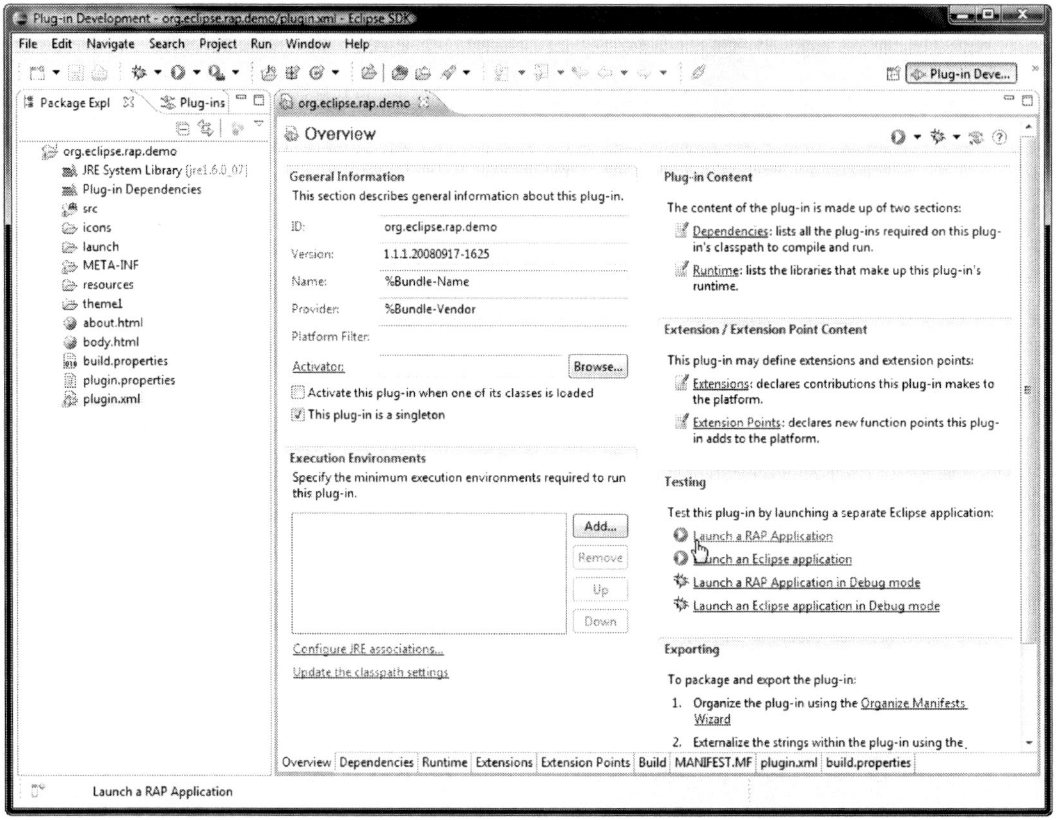

To launch the application, select Launch a RAP Application from the "Testing" tab. The application will start up by starting an integrated Jetty web server and showing some startup output in the console.

The integrated browser will open up, showing the URL `http://127`
`.0.0.1:50131/rap?startup=default`.

Note   The port number will vary, as it is automatically determined from the list of available free ports. It can be fixed in the Launch dialog.

A blue gradient background will show for a second or two, which is the time required for the browser to load the JavaScript libraries. The user interface depicted in Figure 4-5 will be shown once they are loaded and the application state is synchronized with the server side.

Figure 4-5. The Eclipse RAP sample application

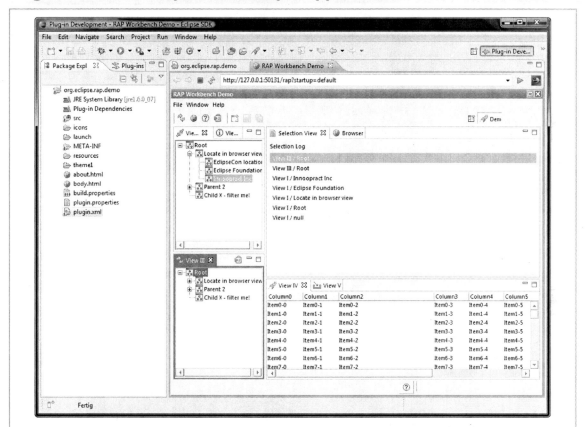

Feel free to play around a bit to get familiar with what RAP and RCP can offer in terms of layout, widgets, and interaction functionality. It is a good idea to compare the effort that would be required using other frameworks to create this functionality with the ease of development in RAP.

INTEGRATED BROWSER

While the integrated browser works OK, sometimes it can be handier to use an external browser (e.g., to use Firebug or check browser compatibility).

The browser used by Eclipse can be configured via Window ➤ Preferences. In the Preferences dialog, type **browser** into the box above the tree and select General ➤ Web Browser. The resulting screen allows you to select between the internal browser (which uses the Internet Explorer rendering engine on Windows systems) and an external browser. If your preferred browser is not autodetected, you can add it using the New dialog.

Creating a Simple Application

After having successfully launched the RAP example application, you'll now try to create your own application from scratch. Instead of using the standard, boring "Hello World" example, we'll create something more useful: a tool with which cats can find new homes and "can openers." It will consist of the Workbench, a view for the general layout, a `TableViewer` to display the cats, and an editor to edit them.

There are different ways to start a new project, and of course also plenty of code to take from the RAP demo project. The goal of this section is to make you familiar with all the involved Eclipse wizards, the fundamental concepts and components, and the usual development workflow.

To start development of a new project, select File ➤ new ➤ Project while in the Plug-in Development perspective. Choose the "Create a new plug-in project" option from the New Plug-in Project dialog. Type in the project name **catshelter**. Also, for the target runtime, make sure to select "an OSGi framework: Equinox," as shown in Figure 4-6.

Figure 4-6. Step 1 in the New Plug-in Project wizard

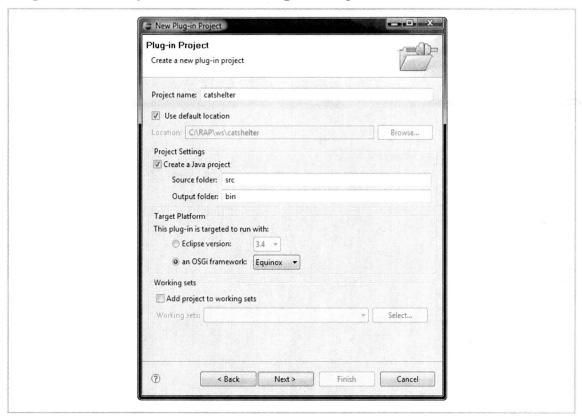

I recommend using the default values proposed for the "Source folder" and "Output folder" options, because this standard convention allows additional tools and plug-ins to integrate more nicely.

If you want, you can change the location of the project by unchecking the "Use default location" check box and using a new path for Location.

Click Next and uncheck "Generate an activator, a Java class that controls the plug-in's life cycle" on the next screen (see Figure 4-7). You are free to edit any other plug-in properties, but that is not required.

Figure 4-7. Step 2 in the New Plug-in Project wizard

After the project has been created, Eclipse will display the plug-in configuration editor. It is similar to the one shown in the RAP sample application in Figure 4-4. I recommend checking the box "This plug-in is a singleton," which will prevent multiple startup of this plug-in.

The project needs to know that it depends on the RAP platform. To tell it that, select the Dependencies tab in the open editor and click Add to add two dependencies:

- `org.eclipse.rap.ui`
- `org.eclipse.rap.ui.views`

Creating an Entry Point

Next, you need to create an entry point, which is responsible for creating the Workbench and a window, and starting them.

To do so, switch back to the plug-in Overview page and select the Extensions link on the right-hand side. Eclipse might ask you to display hidden configuration pages—if so, choose Yes. Then, on the Extensions tab, click Add and enter the following:

```
org.eclipse.rap.ui.entrypoint
```

After that, enter a value that identifies this entry point, like `catshelter .entrypoint1`, and a short name used for the URL to launch the application—for example, `cats`—into the field named parameter, as shown in Figure 4-8.

Note   This name is used to store certain project-related information on the server. If you have run the default configuration from the demo application, reusing the default will bring up some strange errors, like RAP being unable to restore the Workbench layout.

Figure 4-8. Creating the entry point for your application

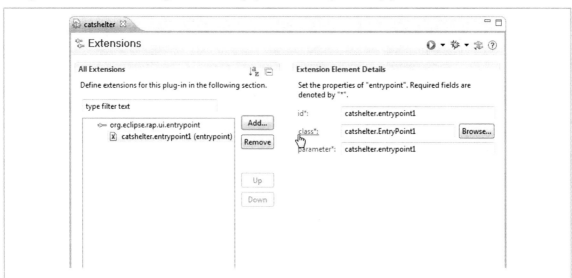

Click the class*: link on the right to open an editor to create this
Entrypoint class. Use the package catshelter and name it
CatEntrypoint

Write the following code for the createUI() method:

```
public int createUI() {
   Display display = PlatformUI.createDisplay();
   WorkbenchAdvisor advisor = new CatWorkbenchAdvisor();
   return PlatformUI.createAndRunWorkbench(display,
       advisor);
}
```

Creating a WorkbenchAdvisor

Next, you need to create the CatWorkbenchAdvisor class, which was
referenced in the createUI() method and is currently shown by Eclipse as
compile error, because it does not yet exist. A WorkbenchAdvisor is
required to initialize some setup parameters, especially the active
perspective, and provide initial layout configuration.

To fix the compilation error, you create that advisor—for example, by selecting that line and pressing Ctrl+1 (that's a numeric *one*, not a lowercase *L*), using the Eclipse-provided shortcut "Create class CatWorkbenchAdvisor."

The automatically generated class would already be enough to let the application run, as the parent WorkbenchAdvisor class provides some amount of default values. However, the application would be still a bit empty. So in the next step, you are going to create a perspective that can hold your cat management.

That perspective (or to be more precise, the identifier for it) has to be returned by the getInitialWindowPerspectiveId() method of the WorkbenchAdvisor. So edit the generated code to return an ID, represented by a string:

```
public String getInitialWindowPerspectiveId() {
    return "catshelter.perspective1";
}
```

Creating a Perspective

Go back to the Extensions tab in the plugin.xml editor, and add the following:

```
org.eclipse.ui.perspectives
```

Make sure that the ID is catshelter.perspective1, as the IDs from the configuration have to match the hard-coded string ID, as shown in Figure 4-9. You can also change the perspective icon and its name here, but we'll skip that for now.

Figure 4-9. Creating a perspective for your application

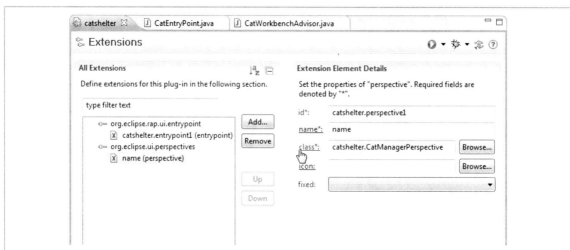

Click the class*: link to open an editor for this perspective.

Again, use the package `catshelter` and the class name
`CatManagerPerspective`. Put in some code that will add a view to your
perspective:

```
public void createInitialLayout(IPageLayout layout) {
   layout.setEditorAreaVisible(false);
   layout.addView("catshelter.view1", IPageLayout.TOP,
      .95f, null);
}
```

The special `Editor` section is not of interest for now, so you set it to be
invisible. You add a view with an ID `catshelter.view1`, and some layout
information that is not relevant for now. Next, you need to create the view.

Creating a View

Again, you need to create an extension in the Extension tab of the plug-in
editor. Click Add and add the extension point:

```
org.eclipse.ui.views
```

This time, no subentry is created by default, as there are three options for that. Right-click the `org.eclipse.ui.views` extension and choose "new" ➤ "view."

As shown in Figure 4-10, give the view the name `CatShelter` and make sure `catshelter.view1` is filled in as the ID, so that it can be linked to your perspective.

Figure 4-10. Creating the view for your application

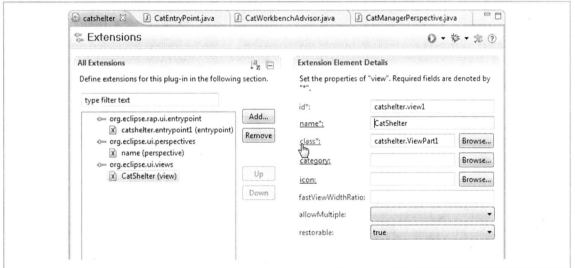

Click the class*: link to open an editor again. This time, use `CatShelterView` as the class name, and also use the package `catshelter`.

Use the following code for the required methods:

```
public void createPartControl(Composite parent) {
   Label helloWorld = new Label(parent, SWT.HORIZONTAL);
   helloWorld.setText("We like Cats!");
}

public void setFocus() {
}
```

When doing the imports, take care that you import `org.eclipse.swt` `.widgets.Label` rather than the AWT label.

The `createPartControl()` method is invoked before that view is created, and you set up its contents here. `setFocus()` can remain empty, as you do not need focus handling right now. The method is required from the `AbstractView` class and intended to let the view decide which subcomponent should receive focus when the view is focused.

Wrapping Up

Before launching the application, let's quickly recap what you've done. There have been plenty of screens and classes, but if you're used to creating RCP applications, this should have been nothing new, as it follows the same model as RCP:

1. Create an `Entrypoint` for RAP to find which `WorkbenchAdvisor` to use. It is an extension of `org.eclipse.rap.ui.entrypoint`.

2. Create a `WorkbenchAdvisor` that specifies which `Perspective` instance to show.

3. Create the `Perspective` that defines which `View` instances are visible. It is an extension of `org.eclipse.ui.perspectives`.

4. Create a `View` class that displays the "We like Cats!" label. It is an extension of `org.eclipse.ui.views`.

This is not that much, actually. I recommend performing a cleanup step, making the string IDs constants of their related objects. By doing so, multiple usage of the same string constant bears less typo risk, and the classes get some editor-recognizable connection. For example, the code should look like this:

```
public class CatShelterView extends ViewPart {
  public static final String ID = "catshelter.view1";
  //...
}
```

```
// and in CatManagerPerspective
public void createInitialLayout(IPageLayout layout) {
  layout.addView(CatShelterView.ID, IPageLayout.TOP,
        .95f, null);
  //...
}
```

Next, you can check what you have created by running your application.

Running the Application

Select Run ➤ Run Configurations from the menu. In the Run
Configurations dialog, select RAP Application from the left-hand panel,
and click the New icon, which is located at the top left and is depicted by a
page with a plus decorator (see Figure 4-11).

Figure 4-11. The Run Configurations dialog

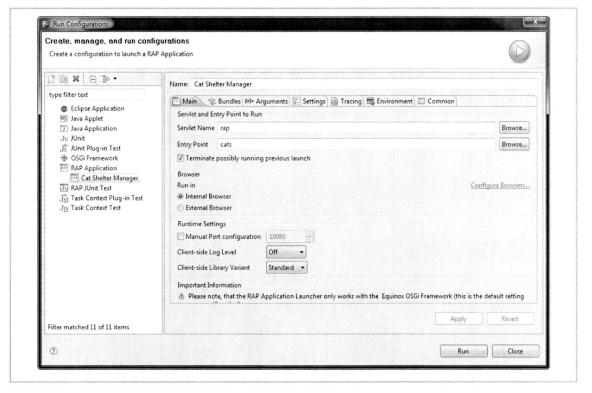

Give this configuration a nice name like Cat Shelter Manager, and choose the entry point by clicking Browse. Click the Run button to see your application starting up, as shown in Figure 4-12.

Note   Depending on your computer speed, Eclipse may open the web browser before Equinox has launched completely and the integrated Jetty server is ready to use. In those cases, a 404 error page will be displayed inside the browser. If this happens, wait a second, and click the refresh button. It should work then.

Figure 4-12. Running your application

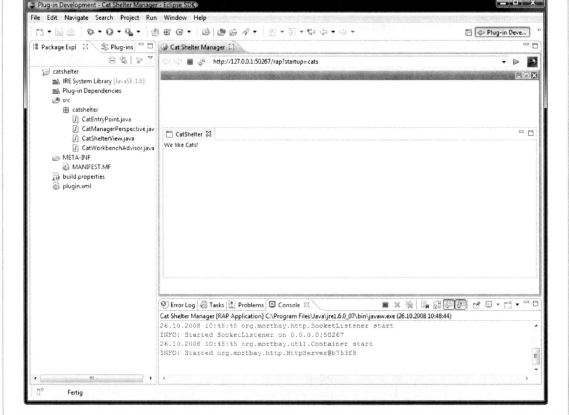

Extending the Application

In this section, we will gradually extend the previous Cat Shelter Manager application. We will use both traditional RCP code and some RAP web influences.

Changing the Window Appearance

Till now, the WorkbenchAdvisor creates a default WindowAdvisor to style the window. To create your own, just overwrite the CatWorkbenchAdvisor#createWorkbenchWindowAdvisor() like this:

```
public WorkbenchWindowAdvisor
        createWorkbenchWindowAdvisor(
          IWorkbenchWindowConfigurer configurer) {
  return new CatWorkbenchWindowAdvisor(configurer);
}
```

Create a CatWorkbenchWindowAdvisor class (preferably using the Crtl+1 shortcut). This class needs one explicit constructor and some code to change the look and feel of the window:

```
public CatWorkbenchWindowAdvisor(
    IWorkbenchWindowConfigurer configurer) {
  super(configurer);
}
public void preWindowOpen() {
  IWorkbenchWindowConfigurer configurer =
      getWindowConfigurer();
  configurer.setInitialSize(new Point(800, 600));
  configurer.setShowMenuBar(true);
  configurer.setShowCoolBar(true);
  configurer.setShowPerspectiveBar(false);
  configurer.setShowProgressIndicator(true);
  configurer.setTitle("Save the cats!");
  configurer.setShellStyle(SWT.TITLE | SWT.MAX
      | SWT.RESIZE);
}
```

The preWindowOpen() hook method is invoked, as the name says, before the window is opened. By default, a RAP application will appear as an application frame inside the browser window. On one hand, this supports the real application look; on the other hand, it might look irritating to see another window in a browser view. As discussed in Chapter 2, a RCP look in a browser window has its usability disadvantages. Also in this default style, it is possible to close the application, leaving the browser empty.

The following code will change this to show the application in the entire browser window:

```
public void preWindowOpen() {
    IWorkbenchWindowConfigurer configurer =
        getWindowConfigurer();
    configurer.setShowMenuBar(true);
    configurer.setShowCoolBar(true);
    configurer.setShowPerspectiveBar(false);
    configurer.setShowProgressIndicator(true);
    getWindowConfigurer().setShellStyle(SWT.NO_TRIM);
}

public void postWindowCreate() {
    Shell shell =
        getWindowConfigurer().getWindow().getShell();
    shell.setMaximized(true);
}
```

Of course, in this case, there is no need to specify an initial size or a title. In the preWindowOpen() method, you set ShellStyle not to have any border. Additionally, you need to set up a postWindowCreate() method callback, as the display area, called shell, needs to be maximized from the initial created state.

As you can see, a MenuBar and CoolBar are defined, but the reserved screen real estate is still empty. That is because neither of these have been filled yet.

Let's fix this in the next step.

Creating a Menu Bar and a Coolbar

To create the menu bar and the coolbar (which Eclipse named as a "cool" version of a toolbar), you need to supply a custom `ActionBarAdvisor` from the `WorkbenchWindowAdvisor`. Do so by providing the following method in `CatWorkbenchWindowAdvisor`:

```
public ActionBarAdvisor createActionBarAdvisor(
     IActionBarConfigurer configurer) {
   return new CatActionBarAdvisor(configurer);
}
```

Create the `CatActionBarAdvisor` and put in the following code:

```
private Action demoAction;

public CatActionBarAdvisor(
    IActionBarConfigurer configurer) {
  super(configurer);
}

protected void fillMenuBar(IMenuManager menuBar) {
  MenuManager windowMenu =
      new MenuManager("Window",
          IWorkbenchActionConstants.M_WINDOW);
  windowMenu.add(demoAction);
  menuBar.add(windowMenu);
}
```

This code declares an `Action` called `demoAction`, and uses it in the `fillMenuBar()` method. For each menu group (e.g., File, Edit, etc.), there should be a `MenuManager`. The constructor takes the label and an identifier. `IWorkbenchActionContstants` already contains some constants for common use cases:

- `M_FILE`: File menu

- `M_EDIT`: Edit menu

- `M_WINDOW`: Window menu

- `M_HELP`: Help menu

`IWorkbenchActionContstants` also holds additional common IDs that can be used. Usage of such standard IDs makes code more readable and frees developers from having to make up their own IDs.

The action is now added to the menu, but it does not exist yet, which you should change. `ActionBarAdvisor` defines a callback designed for creating actions, called `makeAction()`. It also gets a reference to the main window for cross-referencing it in actions.

```
protected void makeActions(final IWorkbenchWindow w) {
  ImageDescriptor demoActionIcon =
      AbstractUIPlugin.imageDescriptorFromPlugin(
          "org.eclipse.rap.ui",
          "icons/full/obj16/font.gif");

  demoAction = new Action() {
    public void run() {
      MessageDialog.openInformation(w.getShell(),
          "Popup", "A simple MessageDialog");
    }
  };

  demoAction.setText("Pop Me Up");
  demoAction.setId("catshelter.popup");
  demoAction.setImageDescriptor(demoActionIcon);
}
```

The code performs three steps:

1. It creates an `ImageDescriptor`, which holds information about the decorating icon used by this action. The icon as such is taken from an already existing plug-in.

2. It creates a new `Action` instance and implements a basic `run()` method that will open a `MessageDialog`.

3. It sets a label, ID, and `ImageDescriptor` to that action.

Once the action is created, it will show up in the menu. As the `CoolBar` can work with exactly the same actions, you can reuse the code for it as well:

```
protected void fillCoolBar(ICoolBarManager coolBar) {
   IToolBarManager toolbar = new ToolBarManager();
   toolbar.add(demoAction);

   coolBar.add(new ToolBarContributionItem(toolbar,
       "toolbar.item1.demoAction"));
}
```

The `ToolBarManager` is a class that takes care of a set of actions that shall be grouped in a toolbar. The `demoAction` is added to a new instance of that class, which is then added to the `CoolBar`, together with an ID, as a `ToolBarContributionItem`.

Creating a Table

Getting back to the essentials of the application, you now need a table that will hold all cats currently seeking a new home. The JFace viewers are ideally suited for this. They are ready-made and can be used for any domain model, by using *providers* to adapt to different models behind them. So let's use a `TableViewer` for displaying some cats. Add the following code to `CatShelterView`, replacing the previous content of that class:

```
private TableViewer viewer;

public TableViewer getViewer() {
  return viewer;
}

public void createPartControl(Composite parent) {
  parent.setLayout(new FillLayout(SWT.VERTICAL));

  Label helloWorld = new Label(parent, SWT.HORIZONTAL);
  helloWorld.setText("Those cats need new can opener");

  viewer = new TableViewer(parent);
  CatLabelProvider labels = new CatLabelProvider();
  labels.createColumns(viewer);
  viewer.setLabelProvider(labels);
  viewer.setContentProvider(new CatsProvider());

  viewer.setInput(getSite());
}
```

The `TableViewer` is stored in a variable and made accessible with a getter so that it can be accessed later. The `Label` is still inside the parent `Composite`, but a layout is required to lay out the components of this view.

Two providers are attached to the `TableViewer`. One, `CatLabelProvider`, is responsible for generating displayable labels out of the domain objects provided by the other provider, `ContentProvider`, named `CatsProvider`. There is one additional call made: `labels.createColumns(viewer)`. This is required for the `LabelProvider` to set up columns in the `TableViewer`, which are filled with some details of the cats being displayed.

To be able to create the `CatsProvider`, first some model classes have to be created in the package `catshelter.model`. Create an `Enum` that represents a cat's gender:

```
public enum Gender {
  male, female
}
```

Next, create a cat model class using the following:

```
public class Cat {
  private String name;
  private String likes;
  private Gender gender;
}
```

Use the source code generation feature from Eclipse to generate appropriate getters and setters for the fields, as well as a constructor from these fields. To access these generators, right-click in the code and select Source ➤ Generate Getters and Setters and Source ➤ Generate Constructor using Fields.

As a replacement for full-blown object storage, you create a singleton that can give you a List of Cat instances. Let's call it CatShelter and place it as well into the catshelter.model package:

```
public final class CatShelter {

  private static CatShelter instance;
  public List<Cat> cats = new ArrayList<Cat>();

  private CatShelter() {
    cats.add(new Cat("Merlin", "running", Gender.male));
    cats.add(new Cat("Mina", "boxes", Gender.female));
    cats.add(new Cat("Meow", "sleeping", Gender.male));
    cats.add(new Cat("Missy", "wool", Gender.female));
  }
```

```
    public static synchronized CatShelter getInstance() {
        if (instance == null) {
            instance = new CatShelter();
        }
        return instance;
    }

}
```

Now all the required model objects are there to create the CatsProvider class in the catshelter.provider package:

```
public class CatsProvider implements
    IStructuredContentProvider {

    public Object[] getElements(Object inputElement) {
        return CatShelter.getInstance().cats.toArray();
    }

    public void dispose() { }

    public void inputChanged(Viewer viewer,
        Object oldInput, Object newInput) { }
}
```

The purpose of an IStructuredContentProvider implementation is to be able to obtain and clean up the data for the viewer. It also provides the means of updating the data. For now, it is enough to return the cats from the CatShelter singleton.

The last and longest class that needs to be created is the CatLabelProvider, which should also go into the catshelter .provider package. It also has to update the TreeViewer to be able to display multiple columns:

```java
public class CatLabelProvider extends LabelProvider
    implements ITableLabelProvider {

  private static final String[] titles =
      { "Name", "Likes", "Gender" };

  public Image getColumnImage(Object element,
      int columnIndex) {
    return null;
  }
  public String getColumnText(Object element,
      int columnIndex) {
    Cat cat = (Cat) element;
    switch (columnIndex) {
      case 0:  return cat.getName();
      case 1:  return cat.getLikes();
      case 2:  return cat.getGender().toString();
      default: return null;
    }
  }
}

  public void createColumns(TableViewer viewer) {
    for (String title : titles) {
      TableViewerColumn column =
          new TableViewerColumn(viewer, SWT.NONE);
      column.getColumn().setWidth(100);
      column.getColumn().setText(title);
      column.getColumn().setResizable(true);
    }
    Table table = viewer.getTable();
    table.setHeaderVisible(true);
    table.setLinesVisible(true);
  }
}
```

The code of getColumnText() is pretty much self-explanatory: it returns the string for the specified column number by accessing different getters.

The `getColumnImage()` method is empty, but could be filled with code returning icons, which would be placed into the cell by the renderer.

The only slightly more complex method is `createColumns()`. It iterates over the static list of column titles and creates a new `TableViewerColumn` for each. It should be emphasized that in JFace, the API uses the object hierarchy, in this case by passing the viewer to the constructor of the additional column, rather than adding additional methods like, for example, `viewer.addColumn()`. This allows cleaner code, but could lead to confusion the first times it is used.

Also, some layout is set up by `createColumns()`, by adding lines and making the headers visible. It could be argued whether that code is correctly placed in this method, or if it should go to some more user interface–related methods; however, adding column titles without making columns that look like columns does not make much sense either. Also note that setting the column width is mandatory; otherwise, the columns would be zero width, because no minimum width is calculated by the renderer (thus making the columns invisible).

Creating an Editor

As a last step, you want to create and use an editor to manipulate the cats displayed in the table. As the editor is an extension of the Workbench, head back to the Extensions tab in the `plugin.xml` editor and add the following:

```
org.eclipse.ui.editors
```

Make sure that the ID is `catshelter.editor` in the screen shown in Figure 4-13, as that ID will be referenced later. Give it the name `catEditor`.

Figure 4-13. Creating an editor

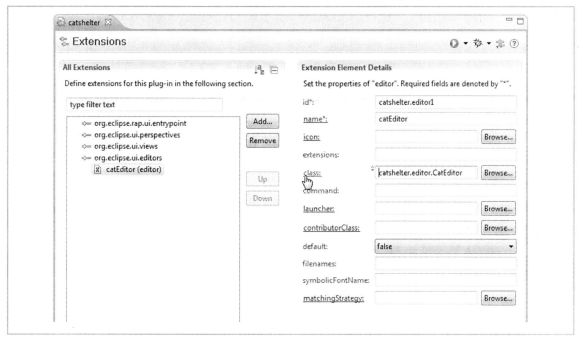

Click the class*: link to open an editor for this editor class.

Use the package `catshelter.editor` and the class name `CatEditor`. For now, only add the ID and fill the `init()` method:

```java
public static final String ID = "catshelter.editor";
private Cat cat;
public void init(IEditorSite site, IEditorInput input)
    throws PartInitException {
  if (!(input instanceof CatEditorInput)) {
    throw new RuntimeException("Input not of type "
        + CatEditorInput.class.getName());
  }
  setSite(site);
  setInput(input);
  setPartName(input.getName());
  cat = (Cat) input.getAdapter(Cat.class);
}
```

The input is checked for compatible type and an adapter is obtained from the input. The adapter pattern is used here to be able to accept different `IEditorInput` objects, but be able to treat them all as a specific domain model classes. Of course, you are free to implement this in another way (e.g., by providing a getter for an instance of `Cat`—but then the input has to be casted and restricted to classes that provide this custom getter).

The `createPartControl()` method is invoked when creating the editor to add the fields for editing. You will add the form editor in the next chapter. Next, you will integrate the editor with the `TableViewer`.

Open the `CatShelterView` class and add two method calls to the end of `createPartControl()`:

```
getSite().setSelectionProvider(viewer);
addEditor(viewer);
```

The `setSelectionProvider()` method call will declare your viewer to be able to tell what is selected in this view. The `addEditor()` method does not yet exist, so you'll create it now:

```
private void addEditor(StructuredViewer viewer) {
    viewer.
     addDoubleClickListener(new IDoubleClickListener() {
       public void doubleClick(DoubleClickEvent event) {
         ISelection selection = getViewer().getSelection();
         if (selection instanceof IStructuredSelection) {

           List selectionList =
               ((IStructuredSelection) selection).toList();
           for (Object selectedObject : selectionList) {

             if (selectedObject instanceof Cat) {
               CatEditorInput input =
                 new CatEditorInput((Cat) selectedObject);
               try {
                 getSite().getPage().openEditor(input,
                     CatEditor.ID);
```

```
        } catch (PartInitException e) {
            throw new RuntimeException(CatEditor.ID
                + " not found");
        }
      }
    }
  }
}
  });
}
```

This code could also be placed directly in `createPartControl()`, but it's generally good practice to encapsulate such functionality in methods. It not only allows reuse of the method code, but also documents what the method does by its name. You add an anonymous implementation of the `IDoubleClickListener` that will be notified when the user double-clicks the viewer. It will invoke the `doubleClick()` method.

The selection is obtained via the `getViewer()` method from the `TableViewer` inside the `CatShelterView`. On the selection, two checks are made using the `instanceof` operator:

1. Is the selection of type `IStructuredSelection`?

2. Is the first object of a possible multiple selection of type `Cat`?

The `instanceof` operator has a nice additional function: it makes sure that the object is not `null`.

To be able to open the editor, first an `EditorInput` object needs to be created and then passed into the `openEditor()` call, which also takes the ID of the editor.

As a last required step for calling the editor, you have to create the `CatEditorInput`, which implements `IEditorInput`. Place it into the `catshelter.editor` package and enter in following code:

```java
public static final String ID ="catshelter.editorInput";

private final Cat cat;

public CatEditorInput(Cat cat) {
  this.cat = cat;
}

public String getName() {
  return cat.getName();
}

public String getToolTipText() {
  return cat.getName() + " likes " + cat.getLikes();
}

public Object getAdapter(Class adapter) {
  return cat;
}
```

The other autogenerated methods can remain empty. Additionally, it is a good idea to generate an `equals()` method to be able to determine the equality of two `EditorInput` instances. To generate it, right-click in the code and select Source ➤ "Generate hashCode() and equals()," and select the `cat` instance member. The `getAdapter()` method is a bit lazy, as it just returns the `Cat` object, but it should be good enough for this example.

Now you can run the application again and double-click a cat in the table view. An editor will open for it and display the cat's name in the tab (see Figure 4-14). Note that opening an editor for the same cat isn't possible, thanks to the `equals()` method of the `CatEditorInput` class.

Figure 4-14. Opening editors for table rows

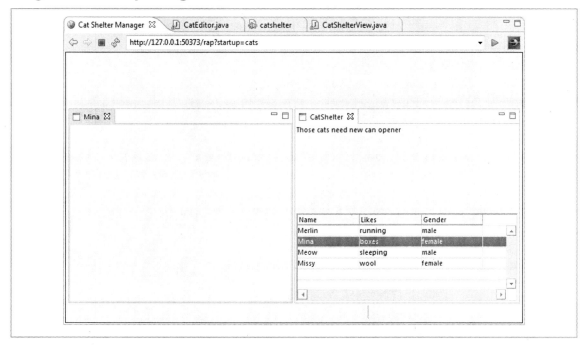

In the next and final section of this chapter, you will add an Eclipse Forms–based editor into the editor view that you opened.

Creating a Form for the Editor

Before you start, you need to add a new dependency to the project. Do so by opening the plugin.xml editor, and switch to the Dependencies tab. Add the following:

```
org.eclipse.rap.ui.forms
```

and save the plug-in configuration.

Now let's edit the createPartControl() method of the CatEditor to set up a form and import the SWT classes (not the AWT ones):

```java
private static final GridData FILL =
    new GridData(GridData.FILL_HORIZONTAL);

private Button male;
private Button female;
private Text name;
private Text likes;
private Button save;

public void createPartControl(Composite parent) {
  FormToolkit tk = new FormToolkit(parent.getDisplay());
  Composite body = tk.createForm(parent).getBody();
  body.setLayout(new GridLayout(2, true));

  tk.createLabel(body, "Name:");
  name = new Text(body, SWT.BORDER);
  name.setLayoutData(FILL);

  tk.createLabel(body, "Likes:");
  likes = new Text(body, SWT.BORDER);
  likes.setLayoutData(FILL);

  tk.createLabel(body, "Gender:");
  Composite group = tk.createComposite(body);
  group.setLayout(new FillLayout(SWT.VERTICAL));
  male = tk.createButton(group, "male", SWT.RADIO);
  female = tk.createButton(group, "female", SWT.RADIO);

  setValuesToFields(cat);

  save = tk.createButton(group, "save", SWT.PUSH);
  save.addSelectionListener(new SelectionListener() {

    public void widgetDefaultSelected(SelectionEvent e){
    }
```

```
    public void widgetSelected(SelectionEvent e) {
        saveValuesToModel(cat);

        IWorkbenchPage page = getSite().getPage();
        IViewPart view = page.findView(CatShelterView.ID);
        if (view instanceof CatShelterView) {
            ((CatShelterView) view).getViewer().refresh();
        }
    }
});
}
```

The `FormToolkit` (stored in the variable `tk` in the code example) has very handy methods for creating things like `Label`, `Field`, and `Button` instances. The very first element created and used as reference for all later elements is the form body. To achieve a nice layout, a two-column grid layout is set for the body.

`Label` and `Text` creation are straightforward. Setting the `FILL` layout to the table cell is just for eye candy, making the field fill the whole table cell.

Note   Storing objects in `private static final` fields conserves memory. You should always consider this if the object can be reused by multiple objects or even multiple threads. Good candidates for that are objects that never change. `GridData`, for example, has no setters, making it immutable.

Contrary to many web frameworks, in SWT, radio buttons are treated the same way as check boxes or regular buttons. The style and behavior is determined by the style attribute passed into the constructor. The `RADIO` type, for example, makes sure that from the buttons in the parent composite, only one is checked.

The fields are updated from the Cat model using a helper method that you will create shortly.

For the save button, you create and add a SelectionListener, which does nothing on the DefaultSelection, but does update the model using a second method you will create on the next page. Most important, it finds and notifies your CatShelterViewer that its TableViewer should refresh itself. This is a simple and efficient method of doing this. More sophisticated solutions would include notification via PropertyChangeListeners.

The methods for setting the values on editor creation and on saving changed values are pretty easy:

```
private void setValuesToFields(Cat cat) {
  name.setText(cat.getName());
  likes.setText(cat.getLikes());
  switch (cat.getGender()) {
    case male:   male.setSelection(true);   break;
    case female: female.setSelection(true); break;
  }
}

private void saveValuesToModel(Cat cat) {
  cat.setName(name.getText());
  cat.setLikes(likes.getText());
  if (male.getSelection()) {
    cat.setGender(Gender.male);
  }
  if (female.getSelection()) {
    cat.setGender(Gender.female);
  }
}
```

Figure 4-15 shows the final application.

Figure 4-15. The final application

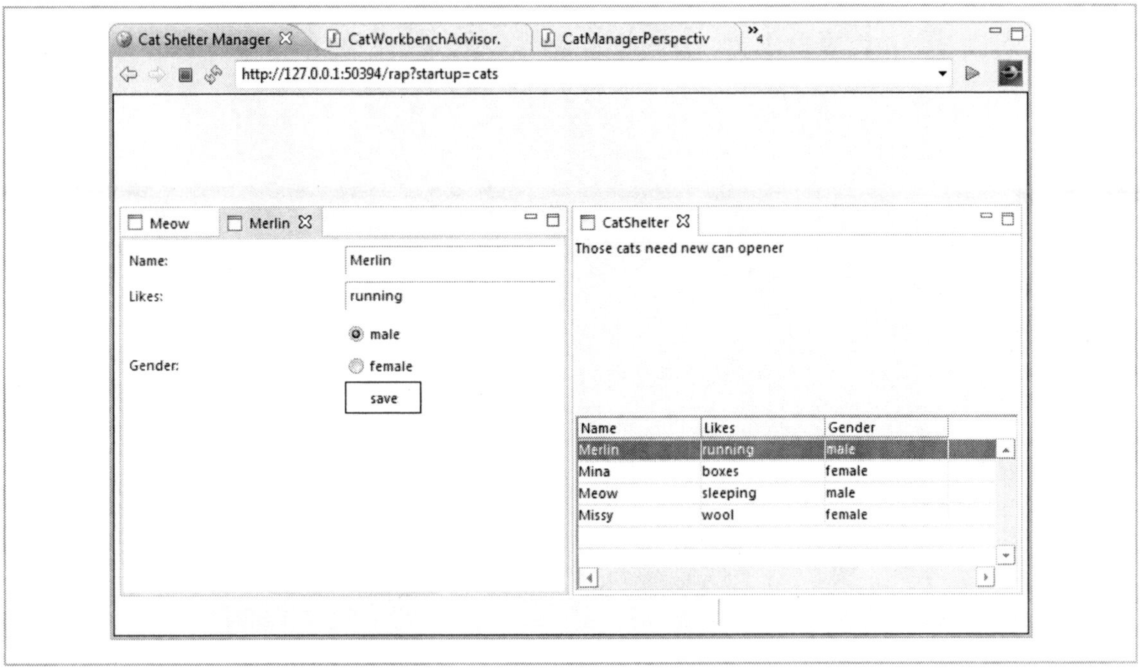

This concludes the creation of a simple RAP application that uses RCP concepts and components.

Chapter 5: Single Sourcing

In Chapter 4, I described how a RAP application can be created and introduced all of the main concepts and components involved in the development of an Eclipse RAP application.

One of the sweet spots of RAP is that it is a technology that aims at making the runtime environment transparent for the developer. Unfortunately, as discussed before, that is not true yet, and perhaps will never be 100 percent true, so the main question answered in this chapter is "How do you either migrate an existing RCP application to RAP or start development of an application that will work fine in both environments?"

This chapter will demonstrate this using a demo application that is available to every Eclipse user, because it is shipped with it: The RCP Mail Client demo. The Cat Shelter Manager application is not used, because it is already based on RAP, but for single sourcing, the existing software isn't. It shouldn't be too hard to apply single sourcing to the Cat Shelter Manager application after studying this chapter.

Pros and Cons of Single Sourcing

Single sourcing is the concept of targeting multiple platforms with the same code base. Java itself is a successful single-sourcing language, as its code can run on virtually every operating system, allowing developers to actually use the concept of *write once, run everywhere*. Single sourcing allows addressing larger markets and user base without spending extra money on development time.

> *"There ain't no such thing as a free lunch."*

> Robert A. Heinlein

But almost every single sourcing has some higher initial costs. It requires some additional skills and testing effort, as from a business perspective, you should not trust the promises of platform providers that want to sell their single-source platform.

In the RAP case, some additional work has to be done to accommodate the existing differences that prevent 100 percent single sourcing. But still, RAP brings in a web view on a client application, which could be a clear competitive advantage.

There are other ideas that can help solve this issue as well. For example, Adobe AIR can run a Flash application as a native desktop application.

For many enterprise applications, Eclipse RAP will take the project or product from where it is already: an Eclipse RCP application in Java. But also for clean slate development, where nothing exists yet, the whole Java-and-Eclipse offering is very compelling, and RAP just completes it. Eclipse RAP makes Java and Eclipse RCP an even more attractive target platform.

Additional testing costs arising from the wish of running the same application on the Web and the desktop should not be neglected. On the other hand, developing a totally new, separate application for the Web would also require testing, and likely even more than in any single-sourcing case.

Actually, with the pure Java language as a base, many projects are limited to a well-defined amount of target platforms. So, the issue of not being able to test every scenario is nothing new, and it is advisable to focus on one environment and from time to time check how the application works in the other. After a while during the project or product development, you may notice that certain functionality just works the same in all of the environments. Testing for these can be reduced, and eventually shifted to more problematic areas. Single sourcing allows delivering a better-quality product to more platforms than when developing for them separately.

Project Setup

To run a successful single-sourcing project, developers have to be able to manage common and distinct code among the different platforms easily. This can be mostly addressed with a sensible setup of the development environment. While some variations of project setup and structure can work fine, the following instructions have proven to be best practice.

A folder schema like this should be used:

```
C:\AppDev\
    - RAP
        - Source
        - Target
        - WS
    - RCP
        - Source
        - Target
        - WS
    - Common
        - Eclipse
        - Source
```

As described earlier, RAP development requires a target platform installation, due to incompatibilities with the development environment. This is most likely not true with the RCP application; however, it is generally a good idea to separate the runtime and testing target platform from the development. I recommend fixing the runtime version to a very specific version, doing controlled changes, and testing with that. This setup will completely decouple the development environment from the runtime, allowing developers in the project to work with their favorite version and plug-ins for development without risking any kind of side effects on the project.

It could be possible to launch the application in either RCP or RAP mode from a single workspace; however, that would involve too much reconfiguration. Instead, two workspaces should be used: one for developing and testing the application against RAP, and the other for doing this against RCP.

The main development should happen in the RAP workspace, because RAP uses a limited subset of the RCP API. Developers will be able to recognize the unsupported parts of the RAP API, either by compile errors, or by missing code completion hints when developing. When developing in RAP mode, it is also almost guaranteed that the application will run in RCP. However, it is advisable not to take that for granted. At least every few days the RCP workspace should be opened and the application compiled and tested.

In general, all source code should first go into projects residing in the Common\Source folder. You should move it out whenever you notice that two different implementations are required for RCP and RAP (I will cover techniques for doing that later). Turning this around, after refactoring and changes in RCP- or RAP-specific code, you should check whether it would be possible to move the newly improved code to the Common folder, creating more single-sourced code.

The source code can be arranged in a similar way for a version control system. For example, in Subversion (SVN), it could look like this:

```
\app-project\
   - branches
   - tags
   - trunk
     - RAP
       - rap_adapter
     - RCP
       - rcp_adapter
     - COMMON
       - components
       - views
```

It might be a good idea to prefix or suffix RAP- or RCP-specific projects so that they can be recognized even without their path hierarchy. Such a setup allows different styles of running the development project.

RAP Proof of Concept

The RAP promise is nice, but if you're with a company running a successful RCP application, it might not be worth putting too many resources into proving that this is true. The described project setup allows two project teams to work in parallel. The one works as before with the traditional setup in the RCP world. The RAP prototyping team can then just pick existing plug-ins and combine them with compatibility plug-ins or workarounds to make the application run in RAP. There will be quick wins so that the application can run in RAP mode to a large extent, and some more problematic code that takes longer to get it running. Sometimes it might be advisable to just do an ugly fix to one specific problem to speed up the general migration effort.

As a side effect of this prototyping work, the main RCP code will get better, because it will implicitly be a code review for the existing code base. Misuse of APIs will be noticed by the RAP prototyping team and corrected. Due to that, it is advisable to put a few experienced developers on the RAP prototyping. It is not about learning RAP or mass development, but spotting issues, rechecking architecture, and ensuring consistency.

Enabling RCP Support for a RAP Application

This use case is perhaps not as common as the one before, but some projects do work this way. Let's say the goal is to develop a RAP-based rich web client. It all could be done in either the RAP or the Common folder, but it is advisable not to do this, for two reasons:

- *Changes to proprietary RAP APIs are easier to manage*: Even though it's successful, RAP is still a young project. Some APIs may still change, especially the proprietary ones. Having code using RAP proprietary APIs already separated will help you deal with such change.

- *Requirements change*: A successful RAP application might generate queries for an RCP client. If the project is set up in the way described previously, it is very easy to supply this RCP client.

Developing for Both Platforms at the Same Time

This is the most common use case. Developers will be able to compile the application in a clearly defined environment without spending a lot of time setting up the environment. It also makes it possible for a few experts to concentrate on platform-specific problems while the majority of developers can develop common code on one or the other platform (or on the working one, in case a platform-specific change has broken the other runtime). The real single-sourced code is usually of higher quality.

Running the Mail Demo in RCP

As a first step, you will set up the development environment as discussed previously. Therefore, the Eclipse SDK goes to the following:

```
C:\AppDev\common\eclipse
```

And the workspace will be pointed here:

```
C:\AppDev\RCP\ws
```

You skip the target installation for now, as RCP can also work with the Eclipse integrated target runtime. To create the project, select File ➤ New ➤ Project ➤ Plug-in Project, and use maildemo as the project name.

As you want the source code to be single sourced, you place the project in C:\AppDev\common\source\maildemo.

You use Eclipse 3.4 as the target runtime, and on the next page of the New Plug-in Project wizard, make sure that you select Generate an Activator and "This plug-in will make contributions to the UI." Also, switch the radio button "Would you like to create a rich client application" to Yes.

After doing this, the next page will offer a template called RCP Mail Template. If that template is not listed, check the settings on the previous page, as they influence the available templates.

Click Finish, and the project will open up. It will not contain any errors, and you can launch it right away, by selecting it and choosing Run As ➤ "Eclipse application" from the context menu.

Feel free to play around with it a bit. It looks simple, but actually uses a good deal of RCP features. When you're done playing and ready to begin with the RAP approach, close this Eclipse instance.

Running the Mail Demo in RAP

To run the mail demo application in RAP, just open Eclipse again, this time pointing to a workspace at `C:\AppDev\RAP\ws`.

The workspace is empty, but can be filled easily. Let's import the project you created from the common project. To do so, select File ➤ Import ➤ Project ➤ Existing Projects from File System.

In the dialog that appears, use `C:\AppDev\common\source` as the root folder. The `maildemo` plug-in should then be autodetected and selected for import. If the project imports fine without any errors, the setup is still missing the target runtime.

In this case, select Help ➤ Welcome, and on the page that opens, click the globe icon on the top-left side and select Rich Ajax Platform (RAP).

Select Install Target Platform, and point the directory here:

```
C:\AppDev\RAP\target
```

Check the check box labeled "Switch the target after installation," if it is not checked by default already.

Now Eclipse should detect that `maildemo` will run in RAP, and report 216 errors to you (as shown in Figure 5-1). The next step is for you to fix those errors so that you can run the application.

Note   The number of errors might vary depending on version of Eclipse and/or RAP used. This number is accurate for Eclipse 3.4 and Rap 1.1.1.

Figure 5-1. Errors for the RAP maildemo plug-in

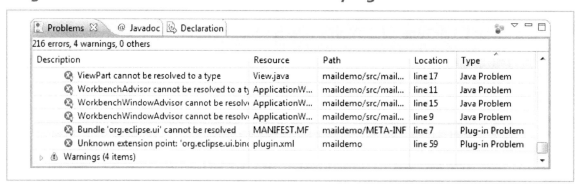

Fixing Imports

It is a good idea to sort by problem type and fix all plug-in problems first, before taking care of any other errors, because many of the errors are likely caused by the plug-in problems.

So, the first error you are going to resolve is this one:

```
Bundle 'org.eclipse.ui' cannot be resolved
```

In fact, the majority of the other problems listed come from missing imports of classes belonging to that bundle. In a RAP target runtime, this bundle does not exist, but there is a replacement provided by RAP that should be used instead. When opening the `plugin.xml` file, this dependency is found on the Dependencies tab.

For an Eclipse RAP target runtime, `org.eclipse.rap.ui` is the bundle you should depend on, because it provides a lot of the missing classes. You will resolve this issue transparently for both the RAP and RCP runtimes.

First, select the dependency `org.eclipse.ui` and click the Properties button. After checking the check box labeled Optional, you can close the dialog and add `org.eclipse.rap.ui` as an additional dependency. After adding this plug-in, you can set the Optional property for it as well.

Save `plugin.xml` and voila: 214 errors gone, 2 left!

Note   Making both bundles optional does the trick but gives a slightly different meaning. If neither dependency bundle is present, the plug-in will not work, despite the fact that both bundles were declared as optional. Also, Equinox will report a missing optional dependency in the log file.

Fixing Extension Points

One of the remaining two errors reads as follows:

```
Unknown extension point: 'org.eclipse.ui.bindings'
```

This extension point exists in the RCP world, but does not exist in RAP. Because there is no replacement for this, you need to get it out of the RAP workspace so that the plug-in can compile.

Because the error comes from a plug-in configuration file, it unfortunately cannot be resolved by regular Java tricks. Instead, you need to use an approach that enables you to distribute the configuration (like the one from the `plugin.xml` file) into plug-ins that can be loaded only on specific runtime platforms.

The preferred solution for resolving such an issue is to create a so-called *plug-in fragment*, which is only activated for the RCP runtime; not for the

RAP one. This works also in reverse for RAP-specific code that might be needed later on and should not be seen in RCP.

PLUG-IN FRAGMENTS

A plug-in fragment is very similar to a plug-in, but the IDE merges the content of the fragment into the parent/host plug-in before launching the application. This causes the classes to exist in the same class loader so that runtime dependencies can be resolved. Compile-time dependencies from the host to the fragment, however, will not work.

To create a plug-in fragment, select File ➤ New ➤ Project ➤ Fragment Project. The Fragment Project wizard will then pop up.

Name this fragment `rcp_maildemo`, place it into the directory `C:\AppDev\RCP\source\rcp_maildemo`, and on the next step, choose `maildemo` as the host plug-in ID.

Cut the extension point for bindings from the `plugin.xml` file of the `maildemo` plug-in, and put it into the `fragment.xml` file of the freshly created `rcp_maildemo` plug-in fragment. The file is created by Eclipse only when needed, but you can also create it yourself.

The `fragment.xml` content should look like this:

```
<?xml version="1.0" encoding="UTF-8"?>
<?eclipse version="3.2"?>
<fragment>
  <extension point="org.eclipse.ui.bindings">
    <key
      commandId="maildemo.open"
      schemeId=
        "org.eclipse.ui.defaultAcceleratorConfiguration"
      sequence="CTRL+2">
    </key>
```

```
    <key commandId="maildemo.openMessage"
      schemeId=
        "org.eclipse.ui.defaultAcceleratorConfiguration"
      sequence="CTRL+3">
    </key>
    <key
      commandId="org.eclipse.ui.file.exit"
      schemeId=
        "org.eclipse.ui.defaultAcceleratorConfiguration"
      sequence="CTRL+X">
    </key>
  </extension>
</fragment>
```

Save it, and you will notice that the compilation error has moved. It is now in the `rcp_maildemo` plug-in, which you are not going to use in RAP, but in RCP. To make sure it does not interfere with the rest of the plug-ins, close the project from its context menu.

Fixing Nonexistent APIs

The last remaining error is the following:

```
ActionFactory.ABOUT cannot be resolved in
ApplicationActionBarAdvisor.java
```

The ABOUT action from RCP doesn't just include a logo and text, but is also able to show plug-in details and the like. Such an action is a bit trickier to do in RAP, and is actually not required for most products, so in this example, you will work around this limitation by creating your own limited ABOUT action.

There are different methods to fix such a problem. One might work better than the other for some cases, so you'll first use one to get the application working, and then move on to the other variants.

First, a new plug-in has to be created, named `rap_compat`. It should go here:

```
C:\AppDev\RAP\source\rap_compat
```

The plug-in needs to depend on `org.eclipse.rap.ui`. After adding the dependency, you create the package `maildemo` and put the class `MyActionFactory` with the following code into it:

```java
public abstract class MyActionFactory {

    private static class WorkbenchPopupAction extends
        Action implements IWorkbenchAction {

      private final String title;
      private final String text;
      private final IWorkbenchWindow window;

      WorkbenchPopupAction(String title, String text,
          IWorkbenchWindow window) {
        super(title);
        this.title = title;
        this.text = text;
        this.window = window;
      }

      public void run() {
        MessageDialog.openInformation(window.getShell(),
            title, text);
      }

      public void dispose() {
      }
    }
```

```
public static final ActionFactory ABOUT =
  new ActionFactory("about") {

    public IWorkbenchAction create(
        IWorkbenchWindow window) {
      if (window == null) {
        throw new IllegalArgumentException();
      }
      WorkbenchPopupAction action =
          new WorkbenchPopupAction("About",
              "We have to build about text here",
              window);
      action.setId(getId());
      action.setText(WorkbenchMessages.get().
                   AboutAction_text);
      action.setToolTipText(WorkbenchMessages.get().
                   AboutAction_toolTip);

      return action;
    }
  };

}
```

That code is to some extent copied from the original SWT source of the
ABOUT action, modified with what is at your disposal from the RAP
runtime.

After saving, you can change line 51 of the
ApplicationActionBarAdvisor class from this:

```
aboutAction = ActionFactory.ABOUT.create(window);
```

to this:

```
aboutAction = MyActionFactory.ABOUT.create(window);
```

After you save, Eclipse now will report a new error:

```
MyActionFactory cannot be resolved
```

This is caused by two settings that have not been changed yet. First, the `rap_compat` plug-in needs to export this package for usage by others. To enable this, open the `plugin.xml` file of that plug-in and go to the Runtime tab. Click the "add" button, select the `maildemo` package, and save.

Second, open the `plugin.xml` file of the main `maildemo` plug-in. On the Dependencies tab, add `rap_compat`. As with the Eclipse user interface plug-ins, make it optional on its properties page to allow the plug-in to start in RCP mode, in which this compatibility plug-in will not exist.

After saving, all compile errors should be gone.

Adding the Entrypoint

Before running `maildemo`, you need to add the `Entrypoint` for RAP. Unfortunately, this is a RAP-specific API. As the `Entrypoint` extension point is defined in the `plugin.xml` file, you should use the same approach as for the bindings extension point (described in the "Fixing Extension Points" section), but this time creating `rap_maildemo` in `C:\AppDev\RAP\source\rap_maildemo`.

Go to the "Extensions" tab and add `org.eclipse.rap.ui.entrypoint`.

Click the class*: link next to the generated class name `rap_maildemo.EntryPoint1` to generate the `Entrypoint` class.

Put the following code into it:

```
public int createUI() {
  Display display = PlatformUI.createDisplay();
  WorkbenchAdvisor advisor =
      new ApplicationWorkbenchAdvisor();
  return PlatformUI.createAndRunWorkbench(display,
      advisor);
}
```

Running maildemo in RAP

From the main menu, select Run ➤ Run Configurations. Select RAP Application and click the New icon on the top left.

Put the ID `rap_maildemo.entrypoint1` into the Entry Point field, and select Apply and then Run.

The application should now show up, working the same way as the original RPC one.

Rerunning the RCP Version

Close Eclipse and switch to the RCP workspace at `C:\AppDev\RCP\ws`. In this workspace, you will now get one compile error and a problem that is not reported by Eclipse, because it is a logical problem.

Because the `rcp_maildemo` plug-in is not yet in the workspace, the bindings extension point will no longer be used by the RCP version of `maildemo`.

To prevent you from forgetting to import it, do it immediately using File ➤ Import ➤ Existing Projects from File System, and using `C:\AppDev\RCP\source\` as the root path to import the plug-in from.

The compile error was caused when you introduced the `MyActionFactory` class for solving the RAP errors. Now you have to do the same for RCP. Create the plug-in `rcp_compat` in `C:\AppDev\RCP\source\rcp_compat`, just as described in the "Fixing Nonexistent APIs" section.

For this plug-in, add the dependency `org.eclipse.ui` and create the abstract class `MyActionFactory` in the `maildemo` package. It can simply extend from `org.eclipse.ui.actions.ActionFactory` and do nothing else:

```
public abstract class MyActionFactory extends
    ActionFactory {

  protected MyActionFactory(String actionId) {
    super(actionId);
  }
}
```

Make sure you export it on the Runtime tab. Now you only have to add the dependency to `rcp_compat`, which you do on the Dependencies tab of the configuration from `maildemo`. It should now list the following dependencies:

- `org.eclipse.core.runtime`
- `org.eclipse.ui` (optional)
- `org.eclipse.rap.ui` (optional)
- `rap_compat` (optional)
- `rcp_compat` (optional)

After saving all files, you can run the application, but you need to update the existing run configuration to include the two new plug-ins on the Plug-ins tab of the run configuration. The last caveat remaining is on the Configuration tab of the run configuration (see Figure 5-2). When making changes to plug-in dependencies, if you don't select the check box labeled "Clear the configuration area before launching," odd errors, such as OSGi not starting due to missing bundles, or runtime exceptions from the RAP code, might occur.

Figure 5-2. The launch configuration

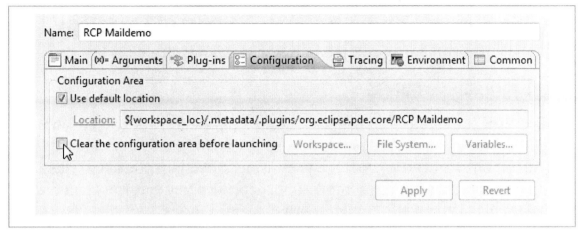

Wrapping Up

While there were many projects and settings involved in making `maildemo` run in RAP and RCP, it resulted in a sound setup. In the end, you created a plug-in fragment for both platforms and a compatibility plug-in for both platforms. With this setup, all issues can be resolved.

Note   When working with two workspaces, it is important to "refresh" the projects after switching workspaces to detect changes on the file system that might be cached by Eclipse. You can refresh projects by selecting them and pressing F5, or choosing Refresh from the context menu. If a clean build of all sources isn't invoked automatically by Eclipse, I recommended performing one. You can do this from the main menu by selecting Project ➤ Clean.

More Single-Sourcing Techniques

In addition to the methods just described, there are still a few variations that might come in handy and provide easier or more elegant solutions.

Using Heavy Reflection

Rather than putting facade code into separate plug-ins (`rap_compat` and `rcp_compat`, in this case), you could also put them in the platform-specific fragment. This, however, would require using reflection to load the class at runtime, rather than having compile-time dependencies that you could have when using a compatibility plug-in that contains the appropriate code. This is because plug-in fragments are merged at runtime only, and thus the classes are not available at compile time. The advantage, however, would be that one platform-specific plug-in fragment would be enough.

Let's try this with your example project. Move the `MyActionFactory` class to the `rap_maildemo` fragment—for example, into the `rap_maildemo` package. Then delete the `rap_compat` plug-in. Eclipse should take care of removing the dependencies where they were referenced before. Now, in the main `maildemo` plug-in, create the `facades` package and put the following class into it:

```
public final class ActionFactoryFacade {
  public static final ActionFactory ABOUT() {
    try {
      try {
        Field f =
          ActionFactory.class.getDeclaredField("ABOUT");
        return (ActionFactory) f.get(null);
      } catch (NoSuchFieldException e) {
        Class myClass =
          Class.forName("rap_maildemo.MyActionFactory");
        Field f = myClass.getDeclaredField("ABOUT");
        return (ActionFactory) f.get(null);
      }
```

```
  } catch (Exception e) {
    throw new RuntimeException(
        "Neither RCP nor custom class worked");
  }
}

}
```

Now you can use

```
aboutAction =
    ActionFactoryFacade.ABOUT().create(window);
```

instead of

```
aboutAction = MyActionFactory.ABOUT.create(window);
```

The reflection code inside this pattern can vary depending on what should be hidden behind this facade. In this case, it is just a static field.

Using reflection in general and exception handling with reflection for specific situations is always a bit tricky. This code might not be 100 percent fail-proof, because reflection calls can throw `SecurityExceptions`, but it works and illustrates the concept.

First, you check if you can get the `static` field from the `ActionFactory`. If it works, you know that you are executing your application against RCP code, or possibly newer RAP code, where this field is implemented.

After introducing this facade, the plug-in `rcp_compat` is no longer required in the RCP workspace, allowing you to clean up a bit more.

The problem with this solution is that the reflection done here is a bit messy and there is actually no visible contract for that interface. The good part of this solution is that it allows graceful enhancements, because it will automatically adapt to new RAP versions that supply the previously unimplemented code.

Using Interfaces and Reflection

You can improve the situation by introducing an interface to better define the functionality. Interfaces also provide better means to refactor method invocations and make code easier to test. This is often the best solution.

As a supplement for the factory you already have in the facades package, let's create an interface there called IActionFactory:

```
public interface IActionFactory {
   ActionFactory ABOUT();
}
```

In both the rap_maildemo and rcp_maildemo plug-ins, you need to create an implementation, and put them into the facades package as well, so you can use a naming convention to retrieve the implementation.

For the RPC version, this is very simple:

```
public class IActionFactoryImpl implements
IActionFactory {
   public ActionFactory ABOUT() {
     return ActionFactory.ABOUT;
   }
}
```

In the RAP workspace, this would look like this:

```
public class IActionFactoryImpl implements
IActionFactory {
   public ActionFactory ABOUT() {
     return MyActionFactory.ABOUT;
   }
}
```

It would of course also be possible to move all code from the MyActionFactory class to the IActionFactoryImpl, but for this example, it should be sufficient to leave it as it is.

The ActionFactoryFacade now can be simplified to the following:

```
public final class ActionFactoryFacade {

  private static IActionFactory INSTANCE;

  public static final ActionFactory ABOUT() {
    if (INSTANCE == null) {
      try {
        Class<? extends IActionFactory> myClass =
            Class.forName("facades.IActionFactoryImpl")
                .asSubclass(IActionFactory.class);
        INSTANCE = myClass.newInstance();
      } catch (Exception e) {
        throw new RuntimeException(
            "Our naming pattern must be broken");
      }
    }
    return INSTANCE.ABOUT();
  }
}
```

This looks a lot nicer and clearer than before. The Java 5 generics pattern also allows better typing support, so you should use it wherever possible. Using a naming pattern, like the facades package and the class name from the interface with the Impl suffix, helps to get code organized, but is not really required.

In both patterns, you can access the ABOUT value as a static field instead of invoking a member method named ABOUT(); however, in the example in which the interface was used, the code is much cleaner:

```
public final class ActionFactoryFacade {

  public static final ActionFactory ABOUT;
  static {
    try {
      Class<? extends IActionFactory> myClass =
          Class.forName("facades.IActionFactoryImpl")
              .asSubclass(IActionFactory.class);
```

```
        ABOUT = myClass.newInstance().ABOUT();
    } catch (Exception e) {
        throw new RuntimeException(
            "Our naming pattern must be broken");
    }
  }
}
```

Note   Static initializers are known for unwanted side effects. Here they only allow you to save two brackets, so you should consider whether they're worth the risk. Especially in the context of a more dynamic class, the class may be loaded before the implementing class is available, resulting in `ClassNotFoundExceptions` that mess everything up.

Creating Unimplemented Classes

APIs that are completely unimplemented by RAP (which means that the complete class does not exist inside the RAP bundles) can easily be implemented in such a way that the single-sourced code compiles. Normally, the intention is to make the API work, but not to its full extent. (If a project might produce a fully functional implementation for a yet unimplemented API, the RAP team will be very happy to accept contributions.)

Let's take the `StyledText` class from SWT. It is a somewhat fancy class that allows text coloration and other visual enhancements for text. Many projects only use `StyledText` for minor visual effects. In these cases, you could easily accept that in the RAP version this styling will be lost, while it remains in RCP deployments.

To illustrate the solution, you will enhance the `maildemo` plug-in slightly.

Let's alter lines 42 and 43 of the `maildemo.View` class from this:

```
l = new Label(banner, SWT.WRAP);
l.setText("This is a message!");
```

to this:

```
StyledText s = new StyledText(banner, SWT.WRAP);
s.setText("This is a styled message!");
StyleRange range = new StyleRange();
range.start = 8;
range.length = 16;
range.fontStyle = SWT.BOLD;
s.setStyleRange(range);
```

In RPC, this executes fine and styles the message title in bold. In the RAP workspace, this will not compile at all, as the `StyledText` and `StyledRange` classes are unknown.

To fix this, you create yet another plug-in, called `rap_supplement`. You make it depend on `org.eclipse.rap.ui`, as you are going to need the SWT `Label` class from there.

Then you create the package `org.eclipse.swt.custom`, where `StyledText` and `StyleRange` come from. Now you are going to create a `StyleRange` class inside that package:

```
public class StyleRange {
   public int start;
   public int length;
   public int fontStyle;
}
```

This class only contains code that makes your code compile; there is no functionality needed. Next, you create the `StyledText` class:

```
public class StyledText extends Label {
   public StyledText(Composite parent, int style) {
      super(parent, style);
   }
```

```
    public void setStyleRange(StyleRange range) { }
}
```

In the original SWT code, StyledText has about 8,500 lines of code
(including comments) and extends the Canvas class. This is obviously a
powerful class, so how can you mock it with four lines? The answer is that
you treat StyledText just as an SWT Label. For each StyledText
method call you might find in your code, you can create an empty dummy
in this StyledText clone that just does nothing. It is a quick fix that can
make loads of source code work in RAP with unaltered code but reduced
functionality.

Depending on your required core functionality, you might be able to find a
way to imitate the functionality. For example, you could insert an asterisk
character where the bold text would be:

```
  public void setStyleRange(StyleRange range) {
    if ((range.fontStyle & SWT.BOLD) != 0) {
      String t = getText();
      t = t.substring(0, range.start)
          + "*" + t.substring(range.start,
                                range.start + range.length)
          + "*" + t.substring(range.start + range.length);
      setText(t);
    }
  }
}
```

Admittedly, this is not the most advanced solution, but it's just meant to
illustrate one option you have when implementing yet unimplemented
APIs.

To make this implementation visible for code outside this plug-in, you have
to declare it as an exported package on the Runtime tab of the plug-in
configuration. After doing that, you can add the rap_supplement plug-in
as a dependency to the maildemo plug-in. Again, you should make it
optional to allow the RCP client to work without it (because it contains an
implementation of StyledText).

Patching RAP

Note   This technique isn't supported by any involved party, nor does it produce good code. However, you might consider using it when you want zero interference with the original code (e.g., for proof-of-concept work).

Instead of creating additional code using facades to fix the nonexistent ABOUT action in the `ActionFactory`, you are going to create a patch for that class that includes an implementation.

First, create a patch fragment the same way as before, giving it the name `rap_patch_workbench`. As the `ActionFactory` is part of `org.eclipse.rap.ui.workbench`, define it as a host plug-in. Now you are contributing to the original RAP Workbench plug-in, rather than creating something stand-alone.

Instead of making a real contribution, you are going to replace the `ActionFactory` class. There are two requirements for doing this:

1. The host plug-in must read a JAR file from the class path and declare itself patchable. The RAP team has done this for their plug-ins by using the manifest entry `Eclipse-ExtensibleAPI: true` and declaring the JAR file to be named `patch.jar`.

2. Your plug-in fragment has to create that `patch.jar` file. This is done on the "Build" tab of the plug-in configuration.

Open the "Build" tab. There is an entry already called . (period), which means that the classes are put on the plain class path. Right-click this entry and select Rename from the context menu. Give it the new name `patch.jar`. Now the build will create the `patch.jar` file.

Now your patch fragment will patch the RAP plug-in and will be able to replace classes. Next, you are going to create that replacement. Create the class `ActionFactory` inside the package `org.eclipse.ui.actions`.

Now this class needs to be filled with the RAP source code. The easiest way to obtain this is by importing the `org.eclipse.rap.ui.workbench` bundle from the Plug-ins view into the workspace as source project. See the "Running the RAP Sample Application" section of Chapter 4 for details on how to do that. Locate the `ActionFactory.java` file inside the `src` folder and copy the whole content of that class over to your freshly created `ActionFactory` class.

Now you can copy the code from `MyActionFactory` (see "Fixing Nonexistent API") into here and save. Take care to leave the original code intact and just add the code from the `MyActionFactory`. During runtime, your replacement class will be used instead of the RAP-provided one. But the Eclipse IDE is not yet aware of that, so references to the newly implemented ABOUT field will still not compile.

To inform the IDE of your patching activities, you have to declare it in the `MANIFEST.MF` file (available via the MANIFEST.MF tab of the plug-in fragment configuration) of the `rap_patch_workbench`:

```
Eclipse-PatchFragment: true
```

Note   MANIFEST.MF files are a bit picky. They must end with an empty newline, and each header has to be on a line on its own.

After doing so the, original source code in
`ApplicationActionBarAdvisor`

```
aboutAction = ActionFactory.ABOUT.create(window);
```

will now compile without problems.

Chapter 6: Advanced RAP Features

This chapter contains some examples of advanced features of RAP and how to use them. These features may or may not be required for a successful RAP-based application, but many are nice to know and provide nifty additions to the RAP framework.

Also contained in this chapter is a description on how to write unit tests that simulate basic user interface behavior that can be viewed while developing test cases (similar to what Selenium offers).

Changing the Look and Feel

The point of the rich web client movement is to enable web users to use near-desktop functionality. However, from a usability perspective, it might be counterproductive to have the exact same user interface on the Web and the desktop. As described in Chapter 2, there are some expectations connected with appearance. If Eclipse RAP is to be adopted broadly, its look and feel must be customizable so that the applications can look more web-like, fresher, and more modern.

RAP has supported theming and styling from day one, but until RAP 1.1, this had been based on a proprietary properties file. Since 1.1, this has been aligned with an open web standard: plain CSS files. RAP now enables styling in an established way, and more important, in a way that HTML designers understand. The point with that, having said initially that developers should not need to understand CSS, is that when it comes to making a RAP application look more web-like and integrate into the corporate web application landscape, it often involves people that know CSS. And it is not that it is an essential part of the development process— the widgets are all there—it is now about fine-tuning appearance. Let's have a look.

Configuring RAP to Use a Different Theme

First, you need to create the theme CSS file. To get started with this example, create a folder called themes in the maildemo project. In order to adhere to single-source concepts, you should do this in the RAP-specific fragment. Inside this folder, you are going to create one folder for each theme, so that you can place icons there as well and still easily manage different themes (but this is not mandatory). Inside the rap_maildemo project used in Chapter 5, this would look like Figure 6-1.

Figure 6-1. File structure for CSS files

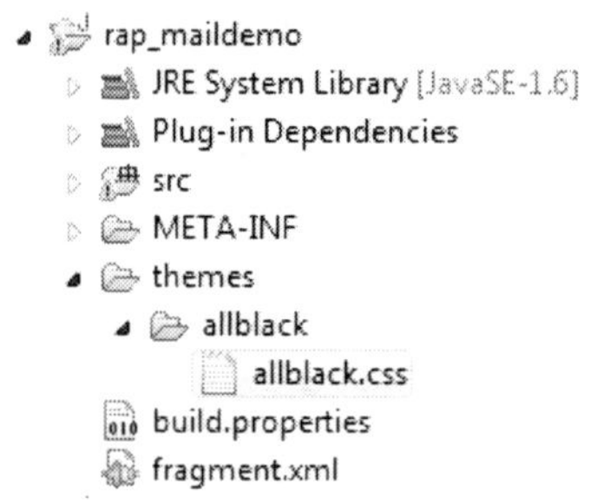

Create a CSS file named allblack.css inside the allblack folder inside the themes folder. The allblack.css file is pretty simple:

```
* {
  color: rgb( 255, 255, 255 );
  background-color: rgb( 0, 0, 0 );
}
```

The * is a CSS2.1 selector that simply applies to every element.

Note   In CSS, all style definitions can either inherit from or overwrite previous definitions. Using global definitions instead of local element definitions can affect the user interface in an unintended way.

SPECIAL RAP CSS

Alongside the CSS2.1 selectors are a few special ones introduced by RAP. The `button` element has, for example, the RAP proprietary attributes `PUSH`, `RADIO`, `CHECK`, and `TOGGLE`, that match the corresponding SWT button style:

```
Button[PUSH] { color: rgb( 0, 255, 0 ); }
```

To apply a CSS class to some widgets in code, RAP supports so-called *variants*:

```
label.setData( WidgetUtil.CUSTOM_VARIANT, "red" );
```

that will match the following:

```
Label.red { color: rgb( 255, 0, 0 ); }
```

To declare the plug-in using this CSS file, you have to specify it using the `org.eclipse.rap.ui.themes` extension point. Create that extension point in the `rap_maildemo fragment.xml` on the Extensions tab, as shown in Figure 6-2.

Figure 6-2. Creating the theme extension

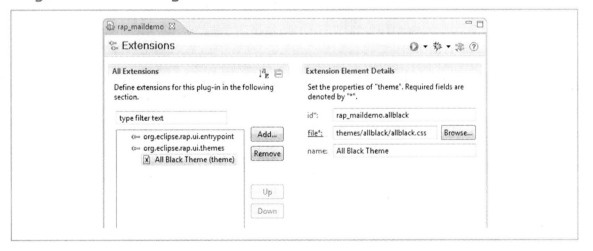

Give it the ID `rap_maildemo.allblack`, and point the file to `themes/allblack/allblack.css`. The name is just used for displaying in this editor, so put something nice here.

Applying the Theme

When you run the application, the theme will not yet be active. That is because just putting files into the plug-in will not trigger any magic. The plug-in needs to be told to use that CSS file. This can be done multiple ways. To efficiently ask RAP to use the different theme, you can pass a reserved parameter called `theme` to the servlet. This parameter will contain the ID of the theme being used:

```
http://127.0.0.1:51034/rap?startup=rap_maildemo.entrypoi
nt1&theme=rap_maildemo.allblack
```

As you can see in Figure 6-3, the mail demo now is pretty much black with white text. Notice that the asterisk selector affects all HTML elements, and destroys some of the original formatting. Generally, it takes some time to develop a good CSS file.

Figure 6-3. Running the All Black mail demo application

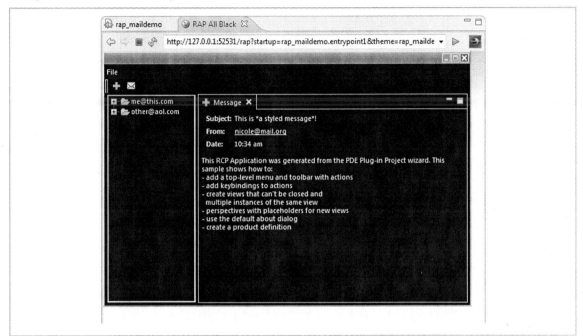

Branding the Application

The process of making an application look like other applications of the same vendor is called *branding*. With branding, certain elements of the corporate brand are put into the application—usually the company name, logo, and colors.

While the previous sections described how to work with coloring, you will now have a look at how to bundle name, logo, and colors together into a branding for the application.

Additionally, the themes extension point has a branding extension point available, called `org.eclipse.rap.ui.branding`. It takes an existing theme extension and combines it with more branding data.

To use the extension, create it in the `rap_maildemo fragment.xml` file on the Extensions tab (see Figure 6-4). The generated ID should be fine, so keep it and fill in the next field, servletName. The servlet name is the identifier for this application. In the previous examples, it was `rap` and was followed by configuration information for the entry point and theme. In this example, a good idea for your servlet name would be `black`. The next two fields save you from giving away the entry point and theme in the URL. This not only makes the URL better looking, but also prevents the user from playing around with it.

For this example, use `rap_maildemo.entrypoint1` for the defaultEntrypointId field and `rap_maildemo.allblack` for the themeId field.

The title field value is displayed as the browser title. Additionally, you could supply an alternate favicon or even a template for the HTML body. That option was created by RAP as an option to supply HTML code inserted into the page—for example, for tracking service snippets. Even more customization is possible using nested `additionalHeaders` elements, which can provide metatags.

Figure 6-4. Creating the branding extension

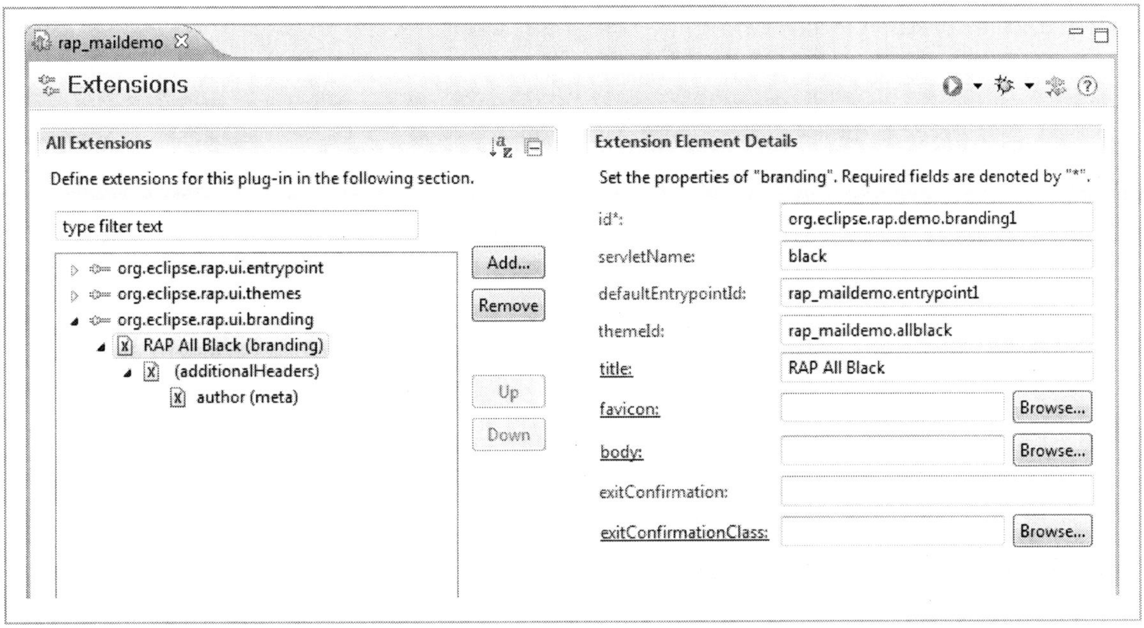

Unfortunately, the RAP application launcher integrated into Eclipse requires an entry point. So the URL opened in the browser by the launcher will be the following:

```
http://127.0.0.1:54158/black?startup=rap_maildemo.entryp
oint1
```

But the startup parameter is actually not required, so removing it and just opening the more user friendly URL

```
http://127.0.0.1:54158/black
```

will also work.

As a last step, you should put any resource files (e.g., CSS files) being used by your plug-ins into the build path, so that binary builds of the plug-ins can work later in deployment (see Chapter 7). To do that, open the plug-in configuration editor of the `rap_maildemo` fragment and switch to the Build tab. On the left side is the project tree shown underneath the label Binary Build. Make sure to select the themes directory.

Note   The RAP team provides a more sophisticated branding example of the mail demo in their CVS repository, dev.eclipse.org:/cvsroot/rt, inside org.eclipse.rap/sandbox/org.eclipse.rap.maildemo.ext.

Writing a Custom Widget

Composition of existing RAP widgets does not allow integrating third-party JavaScript. Especially as today's APIs for rich web clients are mostly in JavaScript, you might need to create an integration widget that can communicate to the third party via JavaScript.

In the following small example, you are going to integrate a basic YouTube player named CatTube into the Cat Shelter Manager application developed in Chapter 4 by creating your own RAP widget.

Creating a Java Widget

The Java side of the widget is very simple. It just holds the YouTube video ID. Let's create the class CatTube in the package catshelter.tube with the following contents:

```
public class CatTube extends Composite {

  private String videoid = "";

  public CatTube(Composite parent, int style) {
    super(parent, style);
  }
  public void layout() {
    // layout done by javascript!
  }
```

```java
    public void setVideoid(String videoid) {
      this.videoid = videoid;
    }

    public String getVideoid() {
      return videoid;
    }

    public Object getAdapter(Class adapter) {
      Object result;
      if(adapter == ILifeCycleAdapter.class) {
        result = new CatTubeLCA();
      } else {
        result = super.getAdapter(adapter);
      }
      return result;
    }
  }
```

And that's it for the widget part on the Java side. Next, you have to create the JavaScript part. The missing class CatTubeLCA and an explanation of it will follow.

Creating a qooxdoo Widget

You must write the JavaScript using the qooxdoo syntax. It is possible to use a different framework, unless it conflicts with qooxdoo. You just need to use the skeleton structure as it is used in the following file. Create the CatTube.js file inside catshelter.tube:

```javascript
qx.Class.define("catshelter.tube.CatTube", {
  extend: qx.ui.layout.CanvasLayout,
  construct: function(id) {
    this.base(arguments);
    this.setHtmlAttribute("id", id);
    this._id = id;
  },
```

```
    properties : {
      videoid : {
        init : "",
        apply : "setVideo"
      }
    },

    members : {
      _doActivate : function() {
        var shell = null;
        var parent = this.getParent();
        while(shell == null && parent != null) {
          if(parent.classname ==
             "org.eclipse.swt.widgets.Shell") {
            shell = parent;
          }
          parent = parent.getParent();
        }
        if( shell != null ) {
          shell.setActiveChild(this);
        }
      },

      setVideo : function() {
        if (this.getVideoid()){
          var t = '<object width="425" height="344">'+
          '<param value="http://www.youtube.com/v/'+
          this.getVideoid() + '" name="movie"></param>'+
          '<embed src="http://www.youtube.com/v/'+
          this.getVideoid()+'" width="425" height="344"'+
          ' type="application/x-shockwave-flash">'+
          '</embed></object>';
          document.getElementById(this._id).innerHTML = t;
        }
      }
    }

} );
```

The first part of this code defines the name for the widget and that it inherits from CanvasLayout. The constructor named construct is a standard one, but it additionally stores the ID into an internal variable. The next section defines the properties of this widget. The Java widget has one property (videoid) that you reflect here. It is initialized with an empty string, and whenever it is changed, the apply method (which you've named setVideo()) is invoked.

Note   qooxdoo will generate getVideoid() and setVideoid() automatically at runtime. Therefore, you should avoid defining getter and setter methods with property names yourself.

The members block lists all the methods available on this object. The _doActivate() method is an internal API callback that registers, for example, focus handling. setVideo() is the function that you set to the apply hook of the videoid property. The majority of your code goes into this. The YouTube API is pretty easy, so you just have to construct an HTML object that will load the Flash video.

Creating a JavaScript-to-Java Connection

Now that you have created the Java and JavaScript sides of the widget, you need to connect them. This is done by a LifeCycleAdaptor (LCA). For SWT, the Java widget is a normal widget that does nothing, because the doLayout() method is empty. But by providing a RAP LCA, you can hook into the various calls made by SWT. To provide the LCA, you have to implement an AbstractWidgetLCA, which is returned by the getAdapter() method in your CatTube widget. Alternatively, you can choose not to implement the getAdapter() method, and instead place the LCA into a package following a very strict naming pattern.

That pattern for the class and package would be as follows:

```
<widgetpackage>.internal.<widgetname>kit.<widgetname>LCA
```

Because this is pretty complex and also provides no navigable connection between the widget and the LCA, you create the class CatTubeLCA and the package catshelter.tube. The following code goes into it:

```java
public class CatTubeLCA extends AbstractWidgetLCA {
  public void renderInitialization(Widget widget)
      throws IOException {
    JSWriter writer = JSWriter.getWriterFor(widget);
    String id = WidgetUtil.getId(widget);
    writer.newWidget("catshelter.tube.CatTube",
        new Object[] { id });
    writer.set("appearance", "composite");
    writer.set("overflow", "hidden");
    ControlLCAUtil.writeStyleFlags((CatTube) widget);
  }
  public void renderChanges(Widget widget)
      throws IOException {
    CatTube tube = (CatTube) widget;
    ControlLCAUtil.writeChanges(tube);
    JSWriter writer = JSWriter.getWriterFor(widget);
    writer.set("videoid", "videoid", tube.getVideoid());
  }
  public void renderDispose(Widget widget)
      throws IOException {
    JSWriter writer = JSWriter.getWriterFor(widget);
    writer.dispose();
  }

  public void readData(Widget widget) {
  }

  public void preserveValues(Widget widget) {
  }

}
```

The `renderInitialization()` method sets up the widget by writing a `newWidget()` method to the JavaScript writer. The ID that goes into the `newWidget()` method call has to match exactly the widget name inside the JavaScript file, and is case sensitive. The second method, `renderChanges()`, is invoked whenever changes from the Java widget need to be passed to the JavaScript widget. It is important not to forget the `ControlLCAUtil.writeChanges()` call, which invokes all the basic widget manipulation, such as layout. The change you actually want to transport is a property change. The `set()` method of the JavaScript writer takes the Java property name and the JavaScript property name alongside the new value. In general, you should use the same name for JavaScript and Java properties, or use constants prefixed with `JAVA_` and `JS_`, to reduce the risk of confusion.

The last method you implement is `renderDispose()`, which takes care of destroying the widget on the client side to reduce memory consumption.

You did not implement `readData()`, which is basically the opposite of `renderChanges()`. It is the hook to obtain data changes on the JavaScript side of the Java widget. You also left out `preserveValues()`, which allows you to store some values in the session for reinitializing the widget when it is recreated after disposing. Neither method is required, because there is no event that you might to want read from JavaScript and transport to the Java side.

Creating a View

Now that you have implemented the widget completely, you can create a view that contains the `CatTube` inside the package `catshelter.tube`:

```
public class CatTubeView extends ViewPart {

    public static final String ID = "catshelter.view2";

    public void createPartControl(Composite p) {
```

```
   p.setLayout(new GridLayout(1, true));
   Composite c = new Composite(p, SWT.NONE);
   c.setLayout(new GridLayout(3, false));
   FormToolkit tk = new FormToolkit(c.getDisplay());
   final Label l  = tk.createLabel(c, "Video ID");
   final Text id  = tk.createText(c, "Wvo-g_JvURI");
   Button b = tk.createButton(c, "view", SWT.PUSH);
   final CatTube tube = new CatTube(p, SWT.FILL);
   b.addSelectionListener(new SelectionListener() {
   public void widgetDefaultSelected(SelectionEvent e){
   }
   public void widgetSelected(SelectionEvent e) {
     tube.setVideoid(id.getText());
   }
   });
  }
  public void setFocus() {}
}
```

The code for this view is pretty straightforward. It creates a small input
area followed by the new CatTube widget. The Wvo-g_JvURI text is the ID
for a funny cat video that you can play after starting the application. After
the user clicks the button next to the video widget, that text will be set to
the widget via the button's SelectionListener.

The usual registration of this view in the plugin.xml configuration on the
Extension tab follows. Add a new extension for org.eclipse.ui.views.
Give it the ID catshelter.view2, the name CatTube, and the class
catshelter.tube.CatTubeView.

Creating a Resource Definition

Currently, the JavaScript file CatTube.js is defined on the class path, but
it is not included in the application. To include it, open the Extensions tab
of the plug-in configuration again. The extension point name is
org.eclipse.rap.ui.resources, and your implementation class should

be named `catshelter.tube.CatTubeResource`. Create that class and put following code into it:

```
public class CatTubeResource implements IResource {

  public String getCharset() {
    return "ISO-8859-1";
  }

  public RegisterOptions getOptions() {
    return RegisterOptions.VERSION;
  }

  public String getLocation() {
    return "catshelter/tube/CatTube.js";
  }

  public boolean isJSLibrary() {
    return true;
  }
  public ClassLoader getLoader() {
    return this.getClass().getClassLoader();
  }

  public boolean isExternal() {
    return false;
  }
}
```

There is nothing special to explain about this class—it basically just provides some information about the resource defined in the extension point. The class also contains the option `RegisterOptions.VERSION_AND_COMPRESS`, which additionally shrinks the JavaScript file. If you use this option without `VERSION`, the file will not be versioned, and browser-caching issues can occur, so I recommend including it.

Note Compression in RAP before version 1.2 M2 did not work correctly. See `https://bugs.eclipse.org/bugs/showbug.cgi?id=247791`.

Integrating the View

The last step required before launching the application is to integrate the view. Currently, it is not showing up because it is not used anywhere. You will fix this by changing the `createPartControl()` method of `catshelter.CatManagerPerspective` to add both views and position them nicely around the editor area:

```
public void createInitialLayout(IPageLayout layout) {
   layout.addView(CatShelterView.ID, IPageLayout.BOTTOM,
        .5f, layout.getEditorArea());
   layout.addView(CatTubeView.ID, IPageLayout.LEFT,
        .5f, CatShelterView.ID);
}
```

After starting the application, everything should work now. And you should be able to play the YouTube video from the embedded player (see Figure 6-5). If the video doesn't come up, the `videoId` might have become invalid over time.

Note The RAP team also provides a complex custom widget example using GMaps in their CVS repository, `dev.eclipse.org:/cvsroot/rt`, inside `org.eclipse.rap/sandbox/org.eclipse.rap.demo.gmaps`.

Figure 6-5. The Cat Shelter Manager with CatTube

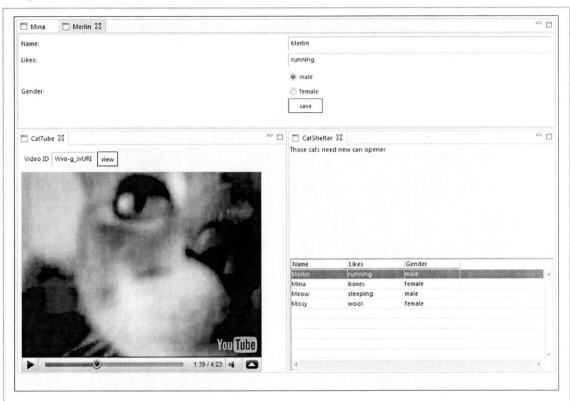

RAP Without the Workbench

Because RAP is very modular, it allows the development of applications that don't use the Workbench concept at all. Even though the main benefit of RAP comes from advanced RCP concepts, it can support some less complex use cases as well. For example, it could allow developers to quickly develop small applications or prototypes.

Instead of using the Workbench and its view concept, you could obtain the Shell element directly in the entry point. The Shell is the main container object to which you can add SWT widgets to.

The following code demonstrates how to use the simple `Shell` to display a basic but easy-to-develop application:

```
public class HelloWorld implements IEntryPoint {

    public int createUI() {
        Display display = new Display();
        Shell shell = new Shell(display, SWT.SHELL_TRIM);
        shell.setSize(300, 300);
        shell.setLayout(new FillLayout());

        shell.setText("Hello World!");

        Label l = new Label(shell, SWT.NONE);
        l.setText("This is very basic");

        shell.open();
        while(!shell.isDisposed()) {
            if(!display.readAndDispatch()) {
                display.sleep();
            }
        }
        return 0;
    }
}
```

This is already enough to be run inside a new plug-in project that has a dependency to `org.eclipse.rap.ui` and this `HelloWorld` class as the extension for the extension point `org.eclipse.rap.ui.entrypoint` defined. When run, the application should look like the one displayed in Figure 6-6.

Figure 6-6. A RAP application without the Workbench

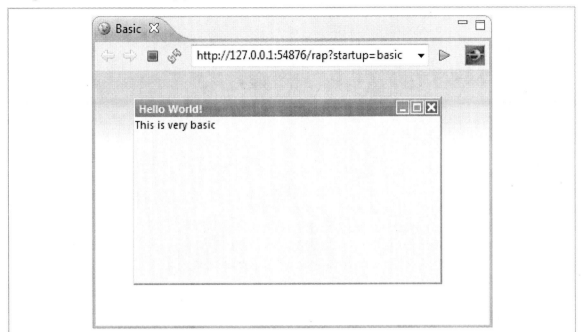

You could also use, for example, the Forms Framework used in Chapter 4 or custom widgets inside the Shell element. The downside of developing like this is that it does not enforce good modularization. But it is also possible to refactor such an application later to use the full Workbench capabilities, because Shell inherits from Composite just as View does.

Unit Testing in RAP

RAP supports standard JUnit testing. It is pretty straightforward. For example, in the Cat Shelter Manager application, you can create the CatShelterTest class inside the catshelter package. You should ideally create this class in a separate SourceFolder called test. The test case you are going to write checks if the application is able to open perspectives successfully. Use the code on the next page for this test case:

```
public class CatShelterTest extends TestCase {

   public void testOpenAndCloseView() {
      openPerspective();
      IWorkbenchPage page = getPage();
      assertEquals(2, page.getViewReferences().length);
      page.hideView(page.getViewReferences()[0]);
      assertEquals(1, page.getViewReferences().length);
   }

   private void openPerspective() {
      IPerspectiveDescriptor descriptor =
       PlatformUI.getWorkbench()
         .getPerspectiveRegistry()
         .findPerspectiveWithId("catshelter.perspective1");
      getPage().setPerspective(descriptor);
   }

   private IWorkbenchPage getPage() {
      IWorkbench workbench = PlatformUI.getWorkbench();
      IWorkbenchWindow window =
          workbench.getActiveWorkbenchWindow();
      return window.getActivePage();
   }

}
```

Note   Currently, the RAP JUnit test runner only supports JUnit 3.x-style test cases. There is no support for annotation-based test cases yet.

This very simple test class inherits from the standard JUnit test case (junit.framework.TestCase). However, it cannot be run using the standard JUnit test case runner. To make the RAP JUnit test runner available, you have to add two additional dependencies to the plugin.xml configuration on the Dependencies tab:

```
org.eclipse.rap.junit
org.eclipse.rap.junit.runtime
```

After saving, you can right-click CatShelterTest and select Run As ➤ RAP JUnit Test. Equinox will start up, followed by Jetty, and the browser will open. This test case should pass, but the application shown by the browser will not look like the one you have created.

Note   Run As ➤ RAP JUnit Test will create a new launch configuration, which by default contains all plug-ins from the workspace and the target platform. To prevent them from interfering, you can adjust the run configuration by deselecting some plug-ins from the Bundles tab.

This is because the Standard JUnit test case does not send user interface updates. But usually when developing test cases that work on the user interface part of an application, it is better to actually see what the test case is doing, and in which state the user interface is when a test is possibly failing.

To deal with this need, the RAP team developed the RAPTestCase. To use it, just replace the extends TestCase with extends RAPTestCase, like this:

```
public class CatShelterTest extends RAPTestCase {
  //...
}
```

When you run the test case again, all the user interface updates done during the tests should be visible in the browser.

Unfortunately, it is not currently possible to run automated headless tests using the RAP test launcher, but tools from RCP can be used for that.

Chapter 7: RAP Deployment

This chapter describes the two scenarios already referenced in Chapter 2:

Running a RAP application inside Jetty inside Equinox

Running a RAP application inside Equinox inside a web container

This chapter will use Tomcat, but other web containers will work similarly.

Running RAP in Jetty in Equinox

The recommended deployment uses an OSGi runtime, which contains a web container. Because OSGi allows easy exchange of bundles during runtime, it is a very good choice for running enterprise applications. Many application servers will become OSGi runtimes in the future, so a framework should be prepared to create OSGi-compatible bundles.

This section describes how to deploy your application to Jetty running in Equinox.

Preparing the OSGi Runtime

First, you need to set up your OSGi runtime. On Windows, create a directory called `C:\rap_deploy\` and a subdirectory called `C:\rap_deploy\plugins\`. Copy from your Eclipse IDE the following directory and two files from the `plugins` directory into `C:\rap_deploy\plugins`:

```
org.eclipse.equinox.launcher.win32.win32.x86_1.0.101. ↪
    R3x_v20080731
```

```
org.eclipse.equinox.launcher_1.0.101.R34x_v20080819.jar
```

```
org.eclipse.update.configurator_3.2.201.R34x_ ↪
    v20080819.jar
```

`org.eclipse.equinox.launcher` is the main OSGi library, and `org.eclipse.equinox.launcher.win32.win32` is just a platform-specific plug-in fragment, which works the same way the `rap_maildemo` fragment works for solving platform issues.

`org.eclipse.update.configurator` looks a bit misplaced, but it takes care of installing all available plug-ins into OSGi.

Note The actual version number will vary depending on your Eclipse version. The first item in the preceding list is a platform-specific plug-in fragment shipped as a directory, not a JAR file.

Additionally, a launcher binary is required. Copy `eclipse.exe` from your Eclipse installation into `C:\rap_deploy` as well. This will be used as a Windows-compatible launcher to start the OSGi Equinox runtime.

As a last step, create `C:\rap_deploy\configuration\config.ini`, a configuration file that will instruct OSGi what to do on startup, and put the following code into it:

```
#Normally the eclipse launcher expects an eclipse app
eclipse.ignoreApp=true

#Do not terminate idle OSGi runtime
osgi.noShutdown=true
#Jetty will use this property to determine the port
org.osgi.service.http.port=7070

#This is what shall be started
osgi.bundles=org.eclipse.equinox.common@2:start, ↵
org.eclipse.update.configurator@3:start, ↵
org.eclipse.rap.ui@4:start,maildemo_feature@4:start, ↵
org.eclipse.equinox.http.jetty@4:start, ↵
org.eclipse.equinox.http.registry@4:start
osgi.bundles.defaultStartLevel=4
```

The osgi.bundles instructions have to go on one line. They tell Equinox to load itself first, and then load the Eclipse helper that will initialize all other bundles. Then RAP will be started, followed by maildemo_feature, which you will create in the next section. Afterward, Jetty is instructed to start. Each bundle is followed by the start level and an instruction on what to do: start. If :start were omitted, the bundle would just be loaded, but not yet activated.

Now, as the directories, plug-ins, and executable are set up and the OSGi platform has been configured completely, you can go ahead and create an OSGi bundle to deploy inside Equinox.

Creating and Exporting a Feature

You will reuse the maildemo plug-in created in Chapter 5. After opening the RAP workspace, you have to create a feature. Select File ➤ New ➤ Other from the main menu, and select Feature Project.

Name the project maildemo_feature, and on the next page of the wizard, mark all plug-ins as required, except RAP demo, RAP, standard JUnit, and any source plug-ins. In total, you should have 31 plug-ins, including the maildemo and rap_maildemo plug-ins (see Figure 7-1).

Note   JUnit is only required for testing, so it is not deployed. Depending on the Eclipse download used, source plug-ins might be made available by the IDE. They would do no harm but increase the size of the deployment package.

Figure 7-1. Selecting plug-ins for the OSGi feature project

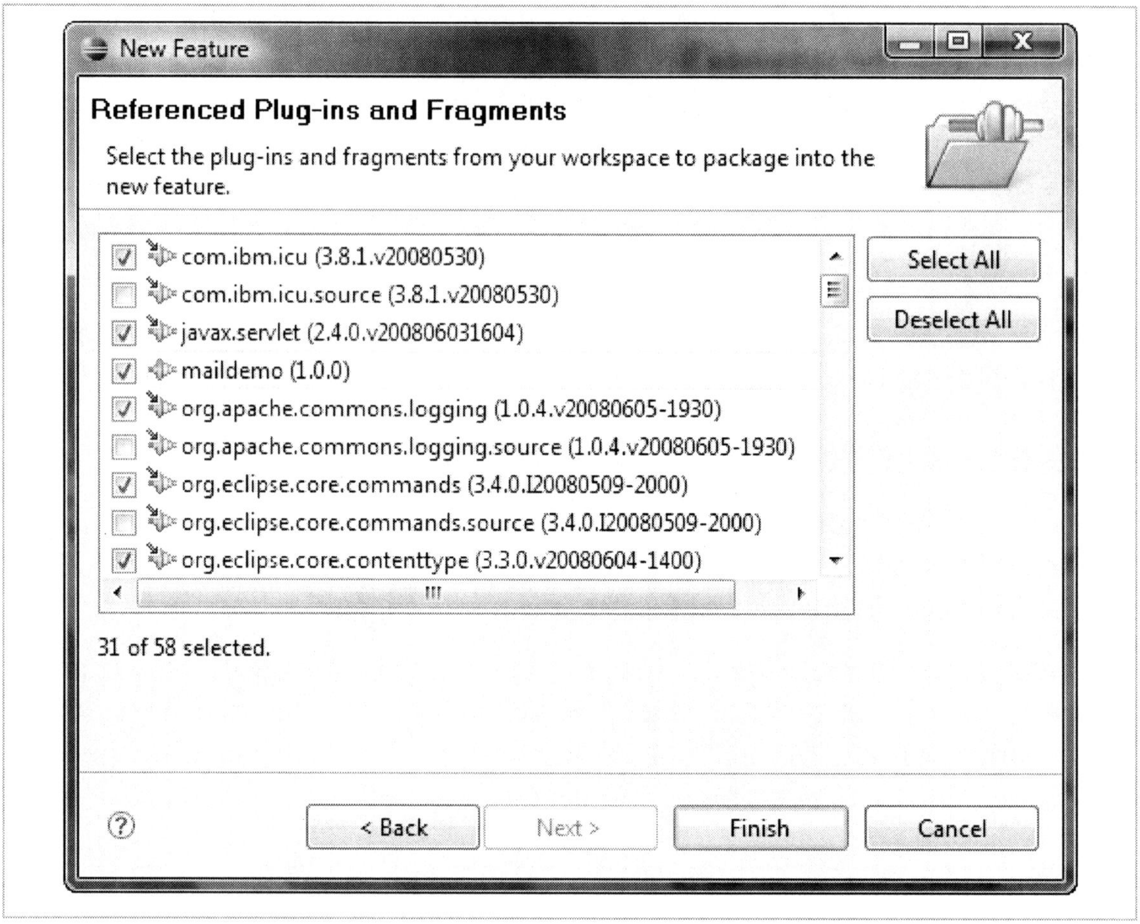

After creation, right-click the `maildemo_feature` project and select Export ➤ "Deployable features."

In the dialog, choose to export to the file system using the path `C:\rap_deploy`. The export wizard will automatically put the plug-ins into the `plugins` subdirectory.

Running the Application in OSGi

Running the application is not very complicated. Just run it from
`C:\rap_deploy`:

```
eclipse -console
```

A new OSGi console will pop up, giving some debug output of Jetty
starting, as shown in Figure 7-2.

Figure 7-2. Equinox startup output

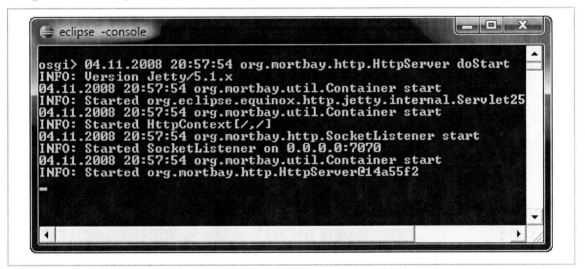

After the startup completes, the application will be accessible via the port
specified in the configuration file. For example, starting the application
with the black theme created in Chapter 6 can be done with the following:

```
http://localhost:7070/black
```

Running RAP in Equinox in Tomcat

Because it is not currently possible with every application server to deploy OSGi bundles directly, this section shows you how to deploy to a web container.

Preparing the Web Container

The sweet spot of running RAP inside a web container is that it is completely transparent for the deployer. By going this way, RAP looks exactly like any other web application.

Any standard web application server can be used. For the next steps, you will use Apache Tomcat, as it is small, free, and widely used. This book assumes that it has been installed to `C:\apache-tomcat-6.0.18`.

There are no additional setup steps required for the application server, but the creation of the RAP web archive is slightly more complicated than deploying OSGi with the integrated Jetty.

Creating and Exporting a Web Archive

Next, you'll create another feature intended to be run in a web archive (WAR).

Name it `maildemo_war` and select the plug-ins the same way as for the OSGi deployment, but make sure to leave out four additional bundles: `javax.servlet`, `org.apache.commons.logging`, `org.eclipse.equinox.http.jetty`, and `org.mortbay.jetty` (see Figure 7-3). You do not need those, as you have an external web container. If you include them, they will cause class-loading conflicts with the classes provided by the web container.

Figure 7-3. Selecting plug-ins for the WAR feature project

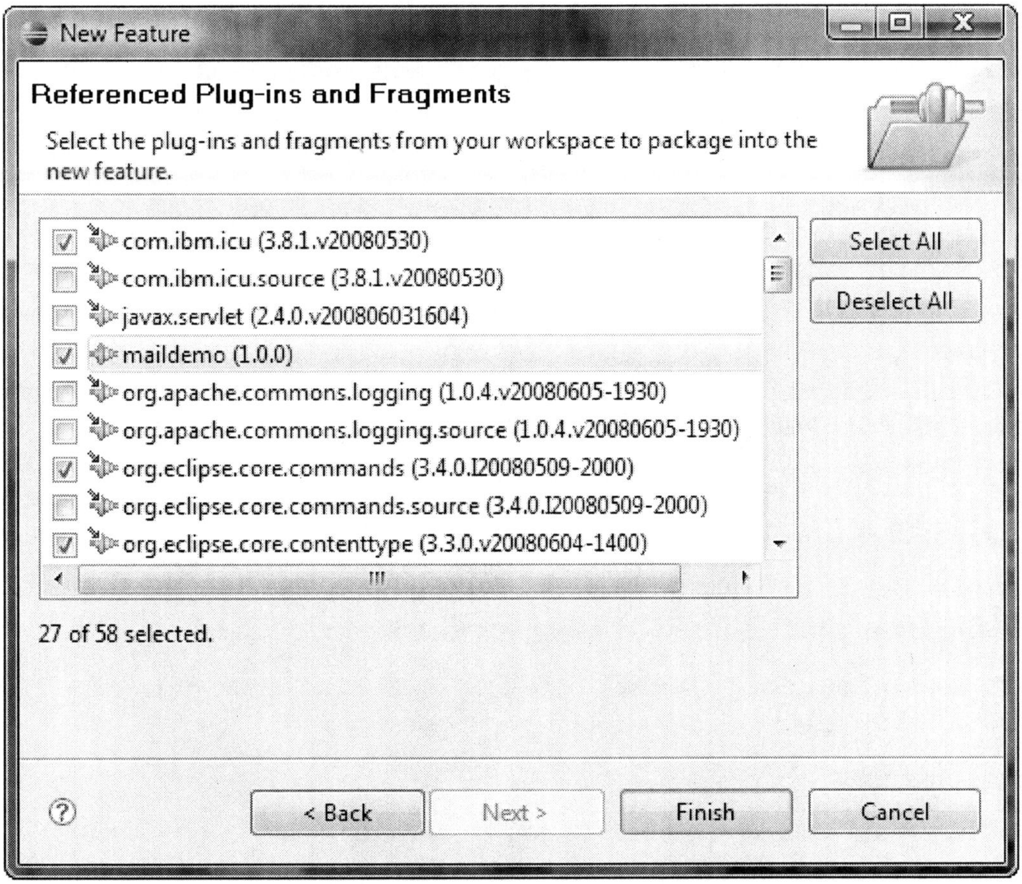

Right-click the feature and select Export ➤ "Deployable features."

In the dialog, export to the file system using the path
`C:\rap_web_deploy\WEB-INF\eclipse`, which you will use to create the
WAR file from. The export wizard will automatically put the plug-ins into
the `plugins` subdirectory correctly.

Next, you need two additional files: `servletbridge.jar` and
`org.eclipse.equinox.http.servletbridge_1.0.0.HEAD.jar`.
Normally, they would need to be compiled from source from the Equinox

project. For convenience, however, they can be downloaded from the book's web site, at `www.rap-book.com/servletbridge.zip`.

The first file needs to go into `C:\rap_web_deploy\WEB-INF\lib` and the latter into `C:\rap_web_deploy\WEB-INF\eclipse\plugins`. Both are responsible for delegating the request from the web server into the OSGi runtime.

Note More information about running Equinox inside a servlet container can be obtained from the Equinox project web site, in the Embedding Equinox in a Servlet Container section, at `www.eclipse` `.org/equinox/server`.

As with the stand-alone OSGi setup, you utilize `eclipse.update` `.configurator` to load all plug-ins as OSGi bundles. Copy the following JAR file from your Eclipse IDE plug-ins directory:

```
org.eclipse.update.configurator_3.2.201.R34x_↪
v20080819.jar
```

to this directory:

```
C:\rap_web_deploy\WEB-INF\eclipse\plugins
```

Create the configuration file for OSGi at `C:\rap_web_deploy\WEB-INF\eclipse\configuration\config.ini` with the following content:

```
osgi.bundles=org.eclipse.equinox.common@2:start,↪
org.eclipse.update.configurator@start,↪
org.eclipse.equinox.http.servletbridge@start,↪
org.eclipse.equinox.http.registry@start,↪
maildemo_war@start
osgi.bundles.defaultStartLevel=4
```

As before, the OSGi bundles need to all go on one line. The last file that needs to be created is web.xml in C:\rap_web_deploy\WEB-INF, which instructs the web container what to do with this WAR.

The contents should look like this:

```
<?xml version="1.0" encoding="UTF-8"?>
<!DOCTYPE web-app PUBLIC "-//Sun Microsystems, Inc.//DTD
  Web Application 2.2//EN"
  "http://java.sun.com/j2ee/dtds/web-app_2_2.dtd">
<web-app id="WebApp">
  <servlet id="bridge">
    <servlet-name>equinoxbridgeservlet</servlet-name>
    <servlet-class>
        org.eclipse.equinox.servletbridge.BridgeServlet
    </servlet-class>
    <init-param>
      <param-name>commandline</param-name>
      <param-value>-console</param-value>
    </init-param>
    <load-on-startup>1</load-on-startup>
  </servlet>
  <servlet-mapping>
    <servlet-name>equinoxbridgeservlet</servlet-name>
    <url-pattern>/*</url-pattern>
  </servlet-mapping>
</web-app>
```

Note   The init-param commandline will activate the console of OSGi to appear in the Tomcat console. When the application works OK and does not need debugging of OSGi bundles any more, you should remove this parameter.

As a last step, you need to actually create the WAR file. Zip the `WEB-INF` folder and name the result `maildemo.war`. Make sure that inside the archive, the first level is `WEB-INF`.

Place this WAR file in the `webapps` folder of the Tomcat installation and start the server. The output will contain the following:

```
INFO: Deploying web application archive maildemo.war
osgi>
```

There will be log output afterward that mixes into the console; press Enter to clear that.

Now you are able to access the application in the port specified by the web container. Additionally, as you have published a WAR, you need to prefix the servlet name with the context root. In case of Tomcat, the context root is the name of the WAR file deployed. For example, you can launch the black configuration from the `maildemo` WAR with the following URL:

```
http://localhost:8080/maildemo/black
```

Note   In case of problems, it is worth checking the log file located in `C:\apachetomcat6.0.18\work\Catalina\localhost\maildemo\eclipse\configuration`.

A very common error is a missing dependency, which can be discovered easily from the log file. For example, it could contain a line like this: `Bundle org.eclipse.update.configurator@start not found`.

Related Titles

Asleson, Ryan, and Nathaniel T. Schutta. *Foundations of Ajax*. Berkeley, CA: Apress, 2005.

Gurumurthy, Karthik. *Pro Wicket*. Berkeley, CA: Apress, 2006.

McAffer, Jeff, and Jean-Michel Lemieux. *Eclipse Rich Client Platform: Designing, Coding, and Packaging Java™ Applications*. Amsterdam: Addison-Wesley, 2005.

McAffer, Jeff, Paul Vanderlei, and Simon Archer. *Equinox and OSGi: The Power Behind Eclipse*. Amsterdam: Addison-Wesley, 2009.

Silva, Vladimir. *Practical Eclipse Rich Client Platform Projects*. Berkeley, CA: Apress, 2008.

Smeets, Bram, Uri Boness, and Roald Bankras. *Beginning Google Web Toolkit: From Novice to Professional*. Berkeley, CA: Apress, 2008.

Library
University of Texas
at San Antonio

Copyright

Eclipse Rich Ajax Platform: Bringing Rich Clients to the Web

© 2008 by Fabian Lange

All rights reserved. No part of this work may be reproduced or transmitted in any form or by any means, electronic or mechanical, including photocopying, recording, or by any information storage or retrieval system, without the prior written permission of the copyright owner and the publisher.

ISBN-13 (paperback): 978-1-4302-1883-8

ISBN-13 (electronic): 978-1-4302-1884-5

Trademarked names may appear in this book. Rather than use a trademark symbol with every occurrence of a trademarked name, we use the names only in an editorial fashion and to the benefit of the trademark owner, with no intention of infringement of the trademark.

Distributed to the book trade in the United States by Springer-Verlag New York, Inc., 233 Spring Street, 6th Floor, New York, NY 10013, and outside the United States by Springer-Verlag GmbH & Co. KG, Tiergartenstr. 17, 69112 Heidelberg, Germany.

In the United States: phone 1-800-SPRINGER, fax 201-348-4505, e-mail orders@springer-ny.com, or visit http://www.springer-ny.com. Outside the United States: fax +49 6221 345229, e-mail orders@springer.de, or visit http://www.springer.de.

For information on translations, please contact Apress directly at 2855 Telegraph Ave, Suite 600, Berkeley, CA 94705. Phone 510-549-5930, fax 510-549-5939, e-mail info@apress.com, or visit http://www.apress.com.

The information in this book is distributed on an "as is" basis, without warranty. Although every precaution has been taken in the preparation of this work, neither the author nor Apress shall have any liability to any person or entity with respect to any loss or damage caused or alleged to be caused directly or indirectly by the information contained in this work.

Printed in the United States
210719BV00003B/19-56/P